IT HAPPENED
IN OREGON

D0055085

IT HAPPENED
IN OREGON

By James A. Crutchfield
Illustrated by Lisa Harvey

TWODOT®

GUILFORD, CONNECTICUT
HELENA, MONTANA
AN IMPRINT OF THE GLOBE PEQUOT PRESS

*To the memory of President James K. Polk,
who brought Oregon into the fold of the United States.*

To buy books in quantity for corporate use
or incentives, call **(800) 962–0973, ext. 4551,**
or e-mail **premiums@GlobePequot.com.**

A · TWODOT · BOOK

Copyright © 1994 by The Globe Pequot Press
Previously published by Falcon Publishing

The publisher gratefully acknowledges the assistance of Terrence O'Donnell
of Portland, Oregon.

Library of Congress Cataloging-in-Publication Data

Crutchfield, James Andrew, 1938-
    It happened in Oregon / by James A. Crutchfield ; illustrated by
Lisa Harvey.
        p.   cm.
    Includes bibliographical references and index
    ISBN 1-56044-290-5
    1. Oregon--History--Anecdotes.   I. Title.
F876.6.C78   1994
979.5--dc20   94-40417
                                                                         CIP

Manufactured in the United States of America
First Edition/Ninth Printing

Preface

This book highlights interesting episodes of Oregon history, from prehistoric through modern times. Each story is complete in itself and can be read individually and out of sequence.

Oregon is an important state historically, and although the vignettes related in this book do not in any way purport to comprise a thorough history of the state, they have been selected to give the reader an understanding of the broad historical background of the Beaver State.

I hope that *It Happened in Oregon* will provide a few hours of pleasure to those who read it, and that it will perhaps find its way into the classrooms of the state, thereby giving younger generations a better appreciation of their vast heritage.

James A. Crutchfield

Contents

CHAPTER ONE

A Baptism of Fire
• 5,000 B.C. •

There was something unsettling about this particular prehistoric day in the vast wilderness that would one day be Oregon. The climate was a bit cooler than it is today, and the forests and open grasslands were inhabited by fauna of the late Pleistocene Period, or Ice Age. Giant mammoths, mastodons, saber-toothed tigers, camels, and the small ancestors of today's horse may well have roamed the region. In their midst loomed the huge volcano now known as Mount Mazama.

Man also made his home here. Armed with spears tipped with finely chipped flint points in the Clovis tradition, he traveled in small bands, following the great animal herds as they ranged from the rich Willamette River Valley in the north to Upper Klamath Lake in the south.

For the past several weeks, these prehistoric hunters had found it unusually difficult to approach their prey. The animals spooked at the least noise or movement. Perhaps, the men thought, this had something to do with recent strange rumblings they had heard coming from the depths of the earth. Then, too, there was the thick, fiery liquid that occasionally oozed from the cone of the volcano.

Even as they discussed these odd events, one of the men pointed frantically to far-off Mount Mazama. Thick smoke billowed from the crest of the peak, and a few moments later the hunters heard a long, loud explosion. As the men and their families watched in awe, the entire mountaintop blew up, belching lava, gas, and ash. The sky darkened and the people were afraid. They fled to a nearby cave and huddled inside, but the dark cloud of ash reached them within minutes. The air smelled terrible, and the landscape was coated in a layer of pumice and lava dust.

For several days, the eruptions continued. The atmosphere grew almost unbearable. At last, the rest of the peak fell into the giant chasm left by the expulsion of millions of pounds of lava.

Thousands of years later, descendants of these ancient Indians still tell the tale of that awful event. The Klamath tribe interpreted the episode as a battle of the gods that lasted for seven days. But if the mythical war only lasted a week, the land took millennia to recover.

The remains of Mount Mazama, which once stretched twelve thousand feet into the sky, today form the basin that holds spectacular Crater Lake. Over the years, as the lava cooled and as rainfall in the area increased, the bowl-shaped depression left by the collapse of the volcano's peak gradually filled with water. Today, Crater Lake is two thousand feet deep, the deepest lake in North America. Nestled like a brilliant blue gem some two thousand feet below the rim of the spent volcano, the lake measures five miles across. Because the water is so clear, moss has been known to grow 425 feet below the lake's surface.

The first known white man to view Crater Lake was a prospector named John Wesley Hillman. When he looked incredulously upon the spectacle in June 1853, he called it the "Deep Blue Lake." Other Americans soon followed Hillman to the rim of the mountain to see one of the natural wonders of the world.

Crater Lake was designated a national park in 1902 by President Theodore Roosevelt. Today, hundreds of thousands of wide-eyed people visit the 200,000-acre park each year. A recent book on the nation's national parks nicely sums up their reaction:

> In a sense, the Crater Lake experience is like the Grand Canyon one—a sudden jolt that comes with discovering you are at the edge of a precipice when you didn't even know the precipice was there. In one lavish crescendo you are simultaneously presented with a

lake five miles across, canyonlike depths, mountainous cliffs, and a natural amphitheater where light and color play lead roles. Visitors seldom react indifferently. Some are astonished. Some step back, uncertain. Few can look away.

CHAPTER TWO

The Claiming of the Columbia
· 1792 ·

On April 17, 1792, George Vancouver made a mistake that may have shaped the destiny of the Pacific Northwest. The British sea captain had been ordered by his government to meet with Spanish authorities about spheres of influence around Nootka Island, known today as Vancouver Island. At the same time, he was to determine whether any great river of the region emptied into the Pacific Ocean.

In 1778, Vancouver's countryman, Captain James Cook, had sailed right by the mouth of the Columbia River in his search for a Northwest Passage—a waterway connecting the Pacific and Atlantic oceans. A Spaniard, Bruno Heceta, thought he may have discovered the "great river" in 1775, but his crew was too sick with scurvy to investigate whether it was a river or a bay. And so it fell to an upstart American to find and name the mighty Columbia and claim it for his country

As Vancouver steered his ship, the *Discovery*, past Cape Disappointment, he noted in his log that

> on the south side of the promontory was the appearance of an inlet or small river, the land behind not indicating it to be of any great extent; nor did it seem accessible for vessels of our burthen, as the breakers extended from the above point, two or three miles into the ocean, until they joined those on the beach nearly four leagues further south.
>
> The Sea had now changed from its natural, to river-coloured water; the probable consequences of some streams falling into the bay, or into the ocean to the north of it, through the low land. Not considering this opening worthy of more attention, I continued our pursuit to the N. W., being desirous of embracing the prevailing breeze.

And so, in a master-stroke of miscalculation, Vancouver bypassed the mouth of the Columbia and left it for the United States to find.

A few days later and only a few miles up the coastline, Vancouver encountered the ship *Columbia*, captained by Robert Gray. A Boston merchant, Gray had frequented these waters for several years, trading with the Indians for luxurious sea otter pelts. On an earlier trip, he had distinguished himself by becoming the first American sea captain to sail around the world. His current trading mission had so far proved successful, despite trouble with hostile Haida Indians in the Queen Charlotte Islands.

Gray and Vancouver arranged to meet aboard one of their ships to discuss the mysterious river that Heceta had described. Gray admitted that he had tried to enter a likely looking inlet several weeks earlier, but to no avail. He also told Vancouver about an ocean inlet to the north, which Vancouver later explored and named Puget Sound after one of his crew. The two captains parted amicably.

On May 11, 1792, Gray made his monumental discovery and described it in his log:

> At half past seven [p.m.], we were out clear of the bars and directed our course to the southward, along shore.... At four, A.M., saw the entrance of our desired port bearing east-south-east, distance six leagues.... At eight, A.M., being a little windward of the entrance of the Harbor, bore away, and run in east-north-east between the breakers, having from five to seven fathoms of water. When we were over the bar, we found this to be a large river of fresh water, up which we steered.... The entrance between the bars bore west-south-west, distant ten miles; the north side of the river a half mile distant from the ship; the south side of the same two and a half miles' distance.

Gray christened the river Columbia in honor of his ship. He and his crew spent the next several days exploring the mouth of the great stream and trading with the friendly natives. John Boit was a fifth mate aboard the *Columbia*, and he left the following account of their encounter with the Indians.

> The beach was lin'd with Natives, who ran along shore following the Ship. Soon after above 20 Canoes came off, and brought a good lot of Furs and Salmon, which last they sold two for a board Nail. the furs we likewise bought cheap, for Copper and Cloth. they appear'd to view the Ship with greatest astonishment and no doubt we was the first civilized people that they ever saw.... at length we arriv'd opposite to a large village, situate on the North side of the river about 5 leagues from the entrance.... The river at this place was about 4 miles over. We purchas'd 4 Otter Skins for a Sheet of Copper,

Beaver Skins, 2 Spikes each, and other land furs, 1 Spike each.

Gray found that the forests lining the Columbia River were rich in game and that the natives were anxious to trade. According to Boit,

> the Indians are very numerous, and appear'd very civill (not even offering to steal). during our short stay we collected 150 Otter, 300 Beaver, and twice the Number of other land furs. the river abounds with excellent Salmon, and most other River fish, and the Woods with plenty of Moose and Dear, the skins of which was brought us in great plenty, and the Banks produces a ground Nut, which is an excellent substitute for either bread or Potatoes, We found plenty of Oak, Ash, and Walnut trees, and clear ground in plenty, which with little labour might be made fit to raise such seeds as is necessary for the sustenance of inhabitants.

Gray and his crew had performed an important service for their country. Five decades later, when the United States and Great Britain would bicker over the placement of the boundary separating their realms, Gray's claim to the Columbia would help ensure that Oregon remained in American hands.

CHAPTER THREE

A Dismal Christmas at Fort Clatsop

·1805·

Christmas Day 1805 dawned gray and gloomy over Fort Clatsop, the nearly completed log stockade that the men of the Lewis and Clark Expedition were constructing on the Pacific Coast. Persistent rain, accompanied by hail, had kept some of the men awake in their huts during the night. At dawn, the sun tried to peek through the clouds, but rain soon resumed for the rest of the day.

Despite the gloom, the men of the expedition did their best to celebrate the holiday. Captain William Clark wrote of their efforts in his journal:

> At day light this morning we we[re] awoke by the discharge of the fire arm of all our party & a Selute, Shoute and a Song which the whole party joined in

under our windows, after which they retired to their rooms were Chearfull all the morning—after brackfast we divided our Tobacco which amounted to 12 carrots one half of which we gave to the men of the party who used tobacco, and to those who doe not use it we make a present of a handkerchief, The Indians leave us in the evening all the party Snugly fixed in their huts—I recved a presnt of Capt L. of a fleece hosrie Shirt Draws and Socks—,a pr. mockersons of Whitehouse a Small Indian basket of Gutherich, two Dozen white weazils tails of the Indians woman, & Some black root of the Indians before their departure.... The day proved Showerey wet and disagreeable.

Captain Meriwether Lewis, co-commander of the expedition, had selected the site for the fort: a sheltered spot near the confluence of the Lewis and Clark and Columbia rivers, in the extreme northwest corner of what is now Oregon. Construction of the fifty-square-foot stockade and several cabins within had begun on December 7. The men named the fort after a friendly local Indian tribe.

The men of the expedition were glad to be settled in one spot for a change. They had explored the northern shore of the Columbia all the way to Cape Disappointment and then crossed to the south side and wandered in the region of Tongue Point before finally choosing a spot for their winter camp.

By January 1, 1806, Fort Clatsop was finished. It was the second camp in which the explorers would spend a winter. The previous year, they had lingered for the season at Fort Mandan, a similar structure they had built along the Missouri River in present-day North Dakota. The group had arrived there in October 1804 after leaving St. Louis in May, and they resumed their journey on April 7, 1805. It had taken the travelers almost eight months to continue up the Missouri River to its headwaters, travel cross-country to the Clearwater River, and then float down the Clearwater to the Snake, down the Snake to the Columbia, and finally down that rushing stream to its mouth at the Pacific Ocean. Now, within earshot of the Pacific surf, they would pass the time until spring, when they would begin the journey home.

While at Fort Clatsop, the expedition members were visited by several tribes of Indians, most of whom were friendly and anxious to help. Game was plentiful, and Lewis, in his journal entry of January 2, 1806, referred to the presence of elk, swans, cranes, beavers, otters, and several species of ducks and geese. Unfortunately, another creature was present in even greater numbers. "The flees are verry troublesom," Clark complained. "Our huts have alreadey Sworms of those disagreeable insects in them, and I fear we Shall not get rid of them dureing our delay at this place."

On January 3, a group of Indians told the men at the fort about a whale that had washed up on shore a few miles away. The Indians presented the expedition with some of the animal's blubber, which Captain Lewis described as

> white & not unlike the fat of Poark, tho' the texture was more spongey and somewhat coarser. I had a part of it cooked and found it very pallitable and tender, it resembled the beaver or the dog in flavour.... Capt. Clark determined this evening to set out early tomorrow with two canoes and 12 men in quest of the whale, or at all events to purchase from the Indians a parcel of the blubber.

According to Clark, when the party reached the dead whale on January 8, the men found

> only the Skelleton of this monster on the Sand between 2 of the villages of the Kil a mox nation; the Whale was already pillaged of every valuable part by the Kil a mox Inds. in the vecinity of whose village's it lay on the Strand where the waves and tide had driven up & left it. this Skeleton measured 105 feet.

On March 23, 1806, the men of the Lewis and Clark Expedition bade Fort Clatsop goodbye and began the long journey home. By the time they reached St. Louis on September 23, 1806, they had traveled more than eight thousand miles through uncharted wilderness. The little camp in which they passed their second winter has been reconstructed based on a diagram drawn by Captain Clark and is now part of Fort Clatsop National Memorial.

CHAPTER FOUR

The Founding of Astoria

· 1811 ·

In April 1811, sixteen men made their way through the damp undergrowth of an evergreen forest to reach some high ground overlooking the Columbia River. They were happy to be on dry land again. They had just come ashore from the *Tonquin*, a 290-ton ship armed with ten guns.

The men's mission was to scout the region for an ideal spot to build a trading post. They selected a place described by one of the builders as "delightfully situated on the Southwest extremity of point George, which is a commanding as well as in every other respect a commodious station." According to Washington Irving, in his classic history, *Astoria*, the men

> now set to work cutting down trees, clearing away thickets, and marking out the place for the residence, storehouse, and powder magazine, which were to be built of logs and covered with bark. Others landed the timbers intended for the frame of the coasting vessel, and proceeded to put them together; while others prepared a garden spot, and sowed the seeds of various vegetables.

Alexander Ross, one of the men who worked on the new post, left behind a harsher account of its construction:

> It would have made a cynic smile to see this pioneer corps, composed of traders, shopkeepers, voyageurs...

all ignorant alike in this new walk of life.... Nearly two months of this laborious and incessant toil had passed, and we had scarcely yet an acre of ground cleared. In the meantime three of our men were killed by the natives, two more wounded by the falling of trees, and one had his hand blown off by gunpowder.

At long last, the workers' task was complete, and as they stood back and looked at their creation—appropriately named Astoria after their employer, John Jacob Astor—they must have considered it a job well done.

Astor was president and majority owner of the recently organized Pacific Fur Company, which intended to make its headquarters at Astoria. At the time of the post's construction, he was in New York City busily running his various other fur interests. With his new company, he planned to challenge the powerful Canadian-run North West Company, which along with its rival, the Hudson's Bay Company, held a monopoly on most of the Pacific fur trade.

Astor's scheme was to send two separate parties, one by land and one by sea, to the mouth of the Columbia River to build the trading post for Pacific Fur. The overland party, led by Wilson Price Hunt and Donald McKenzie, left Montreal on July 5, 1810. After spending the winter of 1810-11 near St. Louis, the group proceeded west and arrived at the site of Astoria on February 15, 1812. Meanwhile, the ocean-going party had set sail from New York on September 8, 1810, and after sailing around the tip of South America in the *Tonquin*, it reached the mouth of the Columbia River a little over a month after the McKenzie-Hunt party.

Soon after the post was completed, the men began hearing rumors of native unrest. On June 5, the *Tonquin*, with twenty-three men aboard, sailed northward to trade with the Indians near Vancouver Island. The ship's departure left only a few men to defend Astoria, and because of the rumors, according to Irving, they suspended their regular labor, and set to work, with all haste, to throw up temporary works for refuge and defence. In the course of a few days they surrounded their dwelling-house and magazines with a picket fence ninety feet square, flanked by two bastions, on which were mounted four four-pounders. Every day they exercised themselves in the use of their weapons, so as to qualify themselves for military duty, and at night they ensconced themselves in their fortress and posted sentinels, to guard against surprise.

In the meantime, they learned that most of the men aboard the *Tonquin* had been massacred by Indians with whom they had been trading. One of the survivors had lured the celebrating natives onto the deserted ship and set fire to the powder magazine. Nearly one hundred Indians were mutilated and killed by the blast. The sailor, too, died in the explosion. Four other crew members who had escaped the massacre were caught by the angry Indians and put to death. An interpreter finally made his way back to Astoria with news of the *Tonquin's* sad fate.

Afraid that an attack on Astoria was pending, one of the partners in the post, Duncan McDougal, resorted to a clever ploy. He called together the chiefs of several neighboring tribes and told them he had heard of the *Tonquin* tragedy and knew of their hostile intentions. Then he pulled a small bottle from his coat pocket and declared,

> The white men among you are few in number, it is true, but they are mighty in medicine. See here, in this bottle I hold the smallpox, safely corked up; I have but to draw the cork, and let loose the pestilence, to sweep man, woman, and child, from the face of the earth!

The Indian leaders, terrified of a devastating smallpox epidemic, fell for the trick and swore eternal peace. McDougal had firmly convinced them that he held their fate in his hands.

After this incident, affairs returned to normal at Astoria. McDougal sent his fur brigades in all directions to trade with the neighboring Indians. But Astor's dream of an American fur empire in the Pacific Northwest was short-lived. In late October 1813, the North West Company, Astor's arch-rival in the region, took over Astoria and all of its furs, furnishings, and supplies, and renamed the post Fort George. After only two and a half years in the fur business, Astoria was no more, but today the city of Astoria sits on the site, a reminder of days gone by.

CHAPTER FIVE

The Ordeal of the Overland Astorians
· 1811 ·

Wilson Price Hunt was a worried man. As he surveyed the boiling rapids of the Snake River on that December day in 1811—standing only a few miles from what is now Ontario, Oregon—he no doubt had second thoughts about this journey he had made.

Hunt conferred with the three Shoshoni scouts who had offered to lead him and his party through the wilderness to the place where the newly created Pacific Fur Company would build its headquarters. He listened carefully to their advice. The Indians wanted to leave the Snake River and travel overland to the northwest, where the party would reach the Columbia River near the villages of the Umatilla Indians.

But why, Hunt inquired, should they leave the river? Why not continue downstream, taking extra care to negotiate the hazardous rapids? The Shoshonis gave a compelling reason. Just a few miles downstream, they explained, the Snake entered a wild and dangerous canyon. There, mighty cliffs towered more than a mile above the river, which was compressed into such a narrow defile that no boat could survive its rapids. The scouts had accurately described the mighty chasm known today as Hells Canyon, a natural wonder that forms the border between Oregon and Idaho.

Hunt was the leader of what has become known as the Overland Astorian party—a group made up primarily of Pacific Fur employees. Although Hunt had little experience for such a task, he had been personally selected by the company president, John Jacob Astor, to steer the group from St. Louis across the Great Plains and Rocky Mountains to the mouth of the Columbia. There, he was to help build a fur-trading post and serve as its business agent.

Hunt left St. Louis on October 2, 1810, accompanied by about sixty men. One of them, an interpreter named Pierre Dorion, had brought along his wife and two children. The party traveled only about 450 miles up the Missouri River before stopping to pitch a winter camp. On April 21, 1811, the expedition resumed its journey, eventually leaving the Missouri and traveling overland.

Hunt's weary party traversed the northern Great Plains and crossed the Continental Divide near what is now Wind River, Wyoming. On September 27, the company reached the Snake River in Idaho and decided to complete its trip on the water. The men cached their saddles, furs, and supplies and built canoes out of the large cottonwood trees that lined the banks of the river.

But the swift Snake proved to be no ally. One man drowned, and several boats overturned and spilled their cargoes. Hoping to increase the chances of meeting friendly Indians who might serve as guides, the party split into several smaller groups.

In early December, Hunt's party encountered one of the other groups, led by Ramsay Crooks, near what is now Homestead, Oregon. Crooks and his men were starving. In the past nine days, they had eaten only a beaver, a dog, a few wild cherries, and some moccasin soles. The two crews united and moved back upriver to a friendly Indian camp. By December 21, Hunt was ready to make the final push to the Pacific.

Hunt finally decided to trust his Shoshoni scouts and set out overland to the Columbia. He and his followers left the Snake at a place known today as Farewell Bend and headed northwestward through Baker Valley, Grande Ronde Valley, and across the Blue Mountains. Thirty years later, this same route would become an important part of the Oregon Trail, the primary highway for immigrants to the Pacific Northwest.

Along the way, at a point near today's town of North Powder, the party experienced still more excitement. Pierre Dorion's wife, Marie, an Iowa Indian, gave birth to a child in the wilderness. Although the newborn died, the remarkable woman summoned the strength and courage to keep up with the rest of the group. Finally, on February 15, 1812—sixteen months after leaving St. Louis—Hunt and his Overland Astorians reached the site upon which they would build the fur post called Astoria.

CHAPTER SIX

A Maiden's Voyage
·1814·

The autumn of 1813 was a sad yet exciting time for the fur trappers and traders at Astoria, headquarters of the Pacific Fur Company. What had first stirred their excitement was the June arrival of the ship, *Albatross*. From its crew, the men learned that the United States and Great Britain were at war. It did not take much imagination to predict trouble here in the Pacific Northwest, where American and British fur companies worked side by side among the Indians.

On October 7, a brigade from the British-owned North West Company arrived at Astoria with the intention of taking over the rival post. It warned the Americans that a warship was on its way to settle the matter by force and offered them the chance to sell out instead. The Astorians had little choice but to accept the paltry sum of $58,000, about a third of the true value of their property, furs, and supplies.

Thousands of miles away, a Scot named Donald McTavish, one of the owners of the North West Company, had recently become acquainted with a beautiful barmaid at a hotel in Portsmouth, England. Since he was on his way to Astoria, and since he had no doubt heard from his associates of the lack of women there, he asked the young maiden, Jane Barnes, to go with him. The pair boarded the ship *Isaac Todd* and sailed across the Atlantic Ocean, around Cape Horn, and up the South and North American coasts to the mouth of the Columbia River.

The approach of any ship was an exciting event at Astoria, which the North West Company had renamed Fort George. It was no different on that day in late April 1814, when the *Isaac Todd* was sighted crossing the sandy bar at the mouth of the Columbia. Workers dropped what they were doing and scurried down to the wharf to meet the ship and see what news its crew might carry. Imagine their surprise when Jane Barnes stepped onto the rough-hewn pier that jutted out into the river!

Ross Cox, one of the men at Fort George, left an account of this memorable day in his book *Adventures on the Columbia River*:

> When the long-expected *Isaac Todd* finally arrived, she brought a cargo of good cheer, new Scottish proprietors, and Doctor Swan who remained as fort physician. She brought delicious cheese, casks of bottled wine, and quantities of English beef to quicken our digestion and refresh our memories of "auld lang syne."
>
> But there was another object brought by the ship that was far more powerful in recalling thoughts of our dear native land. This was Jane Barnes, "a blue-eyed, flaxen-haired daughter of Albion" who was the first white woman to set foot in the Columbia River country. She had been a barmaid in a hotel at Portsmouth where the men had stopped when getting ready to embark on the *Isaac Todd*. In a fit of enthusiasm, she took a dare and decided to make the voyage across the ocean to the great Northwest under the protection of a certain Mr. Mac———.

Miss Barnes caused quite a stir among the men at Fort George. Most of them had not seen a white woman in months—even years—and she must have been an object of great admiration. Cox reported that she was

> beautiful to look upon, lively, and glib in conversation, she gave the first impression of being a person of some education. But when the clerks found her reading a

book upside down, they decided that she was "entirely illiterate and woefully ignorant."

Nonetheless, Jane had many admirers. The local Indians, who had never seen a white woman, were spellbound.

"She was the greatest living curiosity that ever appeared...," Cox wrote. "The red people thronged about the fort in numbers to admire her fair beauty, and to examine with interest every article of her dress."

Jane's wardrobe seemed inexhaustible. Every day, she wore a different outfit, providing constant entertainment for the natives.

Cassakas, the son of the chief of the Chinook tribe, not only admired the fair-haired beauty but wanted her for his wife. One day, Cox reported, the young man

> came to the fort attired in his richest dress, his face fancifully bedaubed with red paint, and his body reeking with whale oil. He had four native wives, but he wanted a white one. He told Jane Barnes that if she would become his wife, he would send one hundred sea-otter skins to her relatives as a present. She would never be asked to carry wood, draw water, dig for roots, or hunt for provisions. He would make her mistress over his other wives, and would permit her to sit at her ease from morning till night. She would wear the clothing that white people wore. Further, she would always have plenty of fat salmon and elk, and would be allowed to smoke as many pipes of tobacco as she thought proper.

Jane would have no part of Cassakas's generous offer, so he finally plotted to kidnap her. When that approach also failed, he refused to frequent the fort ever again as long as Jane was a resident there.

As it turned out, Jane's stay at Fort George was short-lived. When her admirer McTavish drowned while swimming in the Columbia, she had little reason to remain in America, so she set out for her home in England. At Canton, China, she jumped ship, married an English nobleman, and enjoyed all the luxuries that Fort George could not provide.

CHAPTER SEVEN

A Discovery Beneath the Pines

· 1825 ·

David Douglas, a twenty-seven-year-old Scottish naturalist, stood on the deck of the *William and Ann* in 1825 and stared in amazement at the endless forest of evergreens that stretched inland from the rocky Pacific Coast. As his ship tossed in the strong ebb tide at the mouth of the Columbia River, the young scientist looked forward to studying those magnificent trees.

Douglas had come to America at the request of the Royal Horticultural Society of London. His mission was to inventory the species of trees that grew along the coast of the Pacific Northwest and to send specimens back to England. As he studied the coast of what would someday be Oregon, he was particularly intrigued with a type of tall evergreen that dominated the landscape. Later, he would discover it to be a unique species, and it would be named Douglas-fir in his honor.

After disembarking from the *William and Ann*, Douglas prepared to march into the dark, damp forest that covered most of the region between the Pacific Ocean and the western slopes of the Cascade Mountains. Although he was pleased to be on this mission, the young man could not help but experience bouts of discomfiture and loneliness. One night, he wrote in his journal:

> How irksome a night is to such a one as me under my circumstances! Cannot speak a word to my guide, not a book to read, constantly in expectation of an attack [by Indians], and the position I am now in is lying on the grass with my gun beside me, writing by the light

of my Columbian candle—namely, a piece of wood containing rosin!

In late September 1825, Douglas found himself near today's town of Roseburg, Oregon. He broke camp on September 26 hoping to find some of the huge cones of the sugar pine. About an hour out of camp, he met an Indian who "strung his bow and placed on his left arm a sleeve of raccoon skin and stood ready on the defense." Douglas quickly laid his rifle at his feet to assure the brave that he was not hostile. The Indian apparently understood the gesture and, after Douglas gave him some tobacco, he seemed peaceable. Douglas described what happened next:

> With a pencil I made a rough sketch of the cone and pine I wanted and showed him it, when he instantly pointed to the hills about 15 or 20 miles to the south. As I wanted to go in that direction, he seemingly with much good will went with me. At midday I reached my long wished *Pinus*, and lost no time in examining and endeavoring to collect specimens and seeds.

During his search, Douglas found a fallen sugar pine that measured a remarkable 215 feet long and fifty-seven feet in circumference. He could not wait to get his hands on some of the cones of the living pines that towered over his head. But he soon realized that would not be easy.

> Being unable to climb or hew down any, I took my gun and was busy clipping them from the branches with ball when eight Indians came at the report of my gun. They were all painted with red earth, armed with bows, arrows, spears of bones, and flint knives, and seemed to be anything but friendly.

Douglas tried to explain that he was simply collecting pine cones. The natives seemed to understand, but one of them soon began to fidget with his weapons, whereupon Douglas

> went backwards six paces and cocked my gun, and then pulled from my belt one of my pistols, which I held in my left hand. I was determined to fight for life. As I as much as possible endeavored to preserve my coolness and perhaps did so, I stood eight or ten minutes looking at them and they at me without a word passing, till one at last, who seemed to be the leader, made a sign for tobacco, which I said they should get on condition of going and fetching me some cones. They went, and as soon as out of sight I picked up my three cones and a few twigs, and made a quick retreat to my camp.

After several years of "botanizing" in Oregon, California, and Washington, Douglas left the Northwest, but not before he had identified several species of plant life, including the Douglas-fir, the sugar pine, the western white pine, and the magnificent ponderosa pine. He eventually gravitated to Hawaii, where he met a painful death in 1834 when he fell into an underground pit designed to catch wild cattle.

Long after Douglas had gone, his legacy lived on in Oregon. Because of its tough wood, the Douglas-fir quickly became the most popular tree among lumbermen of the Pacific Northwest. Over the next century, millions of board feet would be used to build ships' masts, houses, bridges, and mining tunnels. Today, the species still stands at the top of the lumberman's list of preferred woods.

CHAPTER EIGHT

The Kalawatset Massacre
· 1828 ·

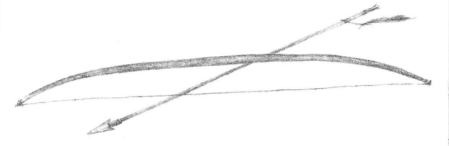

Jedediah Smith and his small contingent of trappers had no idea of the horror that awaited them as they broke camp on July 14, 1828. Along with more than five hundred animal pelts and several hundred horses and mules they planned to sell, the trappers had spent the night on the bank of the Umpqua River near the present-day city of Reedsport, Oregon. As the men extinguished their cooking fires and tended their livestock, Smith prepared to ride ahead to scout out their route. Richard Leland and John Turner would go with him.

Smith has since become known as one of America's foremost explorers and mountain men. According to one of his biographers, Harvey L. Carter, he was the

> first to find and recognize the natural gateway to the
> Oregon country; first overland traveler to reach Califor-
> nia; first to cross the Sierra Nevada; first to traverse the
> Great Basin on its most direct and desert route; first to
> travel overland from California to the Columbia!

For the past few days, as Smith's party had moved up the coastline, it had been harassed by Kalawatset Indians. At the end of a recent trading session, the natives had behaved especially badly. One of the trappers, Harrison Rogers, recorded the event in his diary.

> We found they had been shooting arrows into 8 of our horses & mules, 3 mules and one horse died Shortly after they were shot the Inds. all left camp, but the 2 that acts as interpreters—they tell us that one Ind. got mad on account of a Trade he made and Killed the mules & horses.

Before Smith and his companions left on that fateful July day, he told Rogers not to allow any of the nearby Indians into camp. But Rogers believed that the Kalawatsets were basically friendly. He disobeyed his orders and let about one hundred of the tribesmen come into camp to trade.

The other trappers paid little attention to the Indians strolling around camp. Suddenly, at a given signal, the natives rushed the trappers and killed all but one, Arthur Black. Although severely wounded, Black escaped, and after wandering through the Oregon wilderness for three weeks, he arrived at the gates of Fort Vancouver, about one hundred miles up the Columbia River from the Pacific.

The fort belonged to the Hudson's Bay Company, a British rival of the American trappers. But its chief factor, Dr. John McLoughlin, was not one to refuse a helping hand to any trapper in distress. He later recalled the incident:

> I was surprised by the Indians [who lived around the fort] making a great noise at the gate of the Fort, saying they had brought an American. The gate was opened, the man came in, but was so affected, he could not speak. After setting down some minutes to recover himself; he told us he was, he thought, the only

survivor of 18 men, conducted by the late Jedediah Smith, all the rest, he thought, were murdered.

The next day, McLoughlin sent a small party of friendly Indians to inform the neighboring tribes that he wanted Smith, Leland, and Turner found. To this, he added a stern warning. If Smith and his men were harmed, the Hudson's Bay Company would punish the culprits. To back up his words, McLoughlin armed a forty-man search party, but on August 10, before it could leave the fort, the three Americans arrived.

On September 6, Smith and his two companions left Fort Vancouver with a party of Hudson's Bay men. They intended to go back to the Umpqua River country to try to find their lost goods, as well as any possible survivors of the massacre. The expedition reached the headwaters of the Umpqua on October 10, and the following day, a Kalawatset chief and a few followers rode into camp with several of Smith's horses and mules.

By October 21, the expedition had arrived at the village of the Indians who had perpetrated the massacre. The group demanded the return of Smith's goods. One by one, the Kalawatsets came forth to return 588 beaver pelts, forty-seven otter pelts, and several rifles, cooking pots, and other camp gear and supplies.

The expedition did not succeed in finding survivors. In his journal, McLoughlin wrote that "a Sad Spectacle of Indian barbarity presented itself to our View, the Skeletons of eleven of those Miserabl Sufferers [the massacred trappers] lying bleaching in the Sun."

In the next few days, Smith and his companions recovered more of his goods and animals, including his valuable journals and those of Harrison Rogers.

Although he had survived the Kalawatset massacre, Smith was destined to die at the hands of Indians. On a hot day in late May 1831, the famous mountain man was killed by Comanches on the Santa Fe Trail as he desperately searched for water for companions dying of thirst.

CHAPTER NINE

An Early Excursion up the Willamette
· 1834 ·

In September 1834, Captain Nathaniel Wyeth led a fleet of canoes down the Columbia River on the last leg of a transcontinental journey. A former Boston ice merchant, Wyeth dreamed of building his own fur empire in the Pacific Northwest, competing head to head with the British Hudson's Bay Company. This was his second attempt to fulfill his dream. Accompanying him were several Indians and voyageurs, as well as two scientists, Thomas Nuttall and John Kirk Townsend.

Nuttall was a botanist and curator of the botanical garden at Harvard University. Townsend was an ornithologist. By the time the party neared Fort Vancouver, the two men had collected hundreds of bird and plant specimens, all stored in boxes in the canoes.

A sudden storm buffeted the boats, causing some of them to overturn. Many of Nuttall's prized specimens were soaked. Townsend, in a journal that he later published, described the frantic naturalist's efforts to cope with the disaster.

> He has been constantly engaged in opening [the boxes] and drying them [the contents]. In this task he exhibits a degree of patience and perseverance which is truly astonishing; sitting on the ground, and steaming over the enormous fire, for hours together, drying the papers, and rearranging the whole collection, specimen by specimen, while the great drops of perspiration roll unheeded from his brow.

Fortunately for Nuttall and the scientific community, he was able to salvage most of his collection. The rest of the journey to Fort Vancouver was relatively uneventful.

Townsend left a vivid description of the five-year-old fort, which had been constructed about a mile downstream from an original post the Hudson's Bay Company had already outgrown. In his *Narrative of a Journey across the Rocky Mountains to the Columbia River*, he wrote:

> Fort Vancouver is situated on the north bank of the Columbia on a large level plain, about a quarter of a mile from the shore. The space comprised within the stoccade [sic] is an oblong square, of about one hundred, by two hundred and fifty feet. The houses built of logs and frame-work, to the number of ten or twelve, are ranged around in a quadrangular form, the one occupied by the doctor [John McLoughlin, the post administrator] being in the middle. In front, and enclosed on three sides by the buildings, is a large open space, where all the indoor work of the establishment is done. Here the Indians assemble with their multifarious articles of trade, beaver, otter, venison, and various other game, and here, once a week, several scores of Canadians are employed, beating the furs which have been collected, in order to free them from dust and vermin.

A few days after arriving at the fort, Wyeth, Townsend, and Nuttall took a trip up the beautiful and relatively unexplored Willamette River, looking for an appropriate spot to build a post for Wyeth's fur company.

"At about five miles below the fort, we entered the upper mouth of the Wallammet [sic]," wrote Townsend. "This river is here about half the width of the Columbia, a clear and beautiful stream, and navigable for large vessels to the distance of twenty-five miles."

The men reached the falls of the Willamette on September 30, 1834. Overwhelmed by their beauty and majesty, Townsend wrote:

There are here three falls on a line of rocks extending across the river, which forms the bed of the upper channel. The water is precipitated through deep abrazed gorges, and falls perhaps forty feet at an angle of about twenty degrees. It was a beautiful sight when viewed from a distance, but it became grand and almost sublime as we approached it nearer. I mounted the rocks and stood over the highest fall, and although the roar of the cataract was almost deafening, and the rays of the bright sun reflected from the white a glittering foam threatened to deprive me of sight, yet I became so absorbed in the contemplation of the scene, and the reflections which were involuntarily excited, as to forget every thing else for the time.

Wyeth eventually selected a spot near the mouth of the Willamette for his fur post, but the enterprise was destined to fail. The disappointed Bostonian finally gave up his ambition of becoming a giant in the fur trade and returned to his native city. Nuttall traveled on to Hawaii and California before going home to England, and Townsend served for a brief time as a physician at Fort Vancouver before returning to Philadelphia.

CHAPTER TEN

The Formidable California Cattle Drive
· 1837 ·

In early January 1837, Ewing Young began a journey that he would finish in the saddle, a harbinger of the American cowboy. He left his cabin in the Red Hills of the Chehalem Valley, traveled to Fort Vancouver, and boarded the *Loriot* for the trip down the Columbia River to the Pacific.

Young was a former fur trapper who had scoured much of the Southwest and California for beaver before coming to the Oregon wilderness. There, the Tennessee-born mountain man had settled on some 32,000 acres of prime farmland in the Willamette Valley. He built a distillery and planned to manufacture fine whiskey until disapproving local residents convinced him to change his plans. Instead, he decided to join a delegation interested in bringing beef cattle—woefully lacking—to Oregon from Mexican California. Because of his familiarity with that region, he became the party's leader.

Fierce weather at the mouth of the Columbia delayed the voyage of the *Loriot*, and it wasn't until February 10, 1837, that the mission actually got under way. The ship followed the coastline south to Fort Ross, where passengers were welcomed by the Russian staff. More inclement weather between Fort Ross and San Francisco again slowed the *Loriot*, but on March 1, according to Young's second-in-command, Philip Edwards, the ship arrived "with a fine wind in sight of the entrance of the Bay of San Francisco." The following day, Young went to Monterey to meet with General Mariano Vallejo, commander of the Mexican forces in California. He hoped to negotiate with Vallejo for the purchase of cattle.

But Young received bad news in Monterey. The commander refused to give permission for the cattle drive, saying that only the civil governor, who lived another two hundred miles south at Santa Barbara, had the authority to permit such a transaction.

And so, on March 13, Young set out cross-country to see the governor. By now, the American presence in California had been well-publicized, and in early April a fellow countryman, Faxton Dean Atherton, wrote:

> Capt. Young and Mr. P.L. Edwards of Missouri are now here for the purpose of purchasing cattle to take there [Oregon] if they can get permission of the existing Government to take them from the country. They intend purchasing 600 head and expect to be about 6 weeks on their journey from here to the Columbia, although it can be done in 15 days when unincumbered with cattle, being a good road the whole distance.

To Young's delight, the Mexican governor granted him permission to buy a thousand head of government-owned cattle. By late June, the Oregonians had assembled their herd on the south bank of the San Joaquin River, near today's town of Martinez, California. Not until July 20, however, did they finally swim the stock across the river. Edwards described the arduous cattle drive in his journal:

> Little sleep, much fatigue! Hardly time to eat, many times! Cattle breaking like so many evil spirits and scattering to the four winds! Men, ill-natured and quarreling, growling and cursing! Have, however, recovered the greater part of the lost cattle and purchased others. Another month like the last, God avert! Who can describe it?

The hot days of August were spent moving the cattle northward through the Sacramento Valley. Later in the month, the tired men and animals ascended the Siskiyou Mountains near today's town of Redding. Edwards later recalled the ordeal:

> They appear every day to grow more difficult.... Today the mountains grew more brushy, steep and rocky. To-day we have reached a place where there is water, but no grass. Unless grass is found to-morrow, we have every prospect of starvation to our animals.

By late August, the herd had crossed the boundary separating Mexican California from the Oregon country. Progress was slow, and the men were on the verge of mutiny. Edwards confided in his journal that

> few of our party, perhaps none, would have ventured upon this enterprise could they have foreseen all its difficulties. It boots little to reflect that the future gains will amply compensate for present suffering. Most of the party cursed the day on which they engaged, and would hardly have exchanged a draught of cool water for their expected share of the profits.

Finally, in early October, after an absence of nine months, Young and his men drove the 630 surviving animals into the Willamette Valley, thus providing a basis for the dairy and beef industries in Oregon. The tall, raw-boned Tennessean had succeeded in an undertaking that would not occur on such a vast scale again until the late 1860s, when Texas cowboys would herd their cattle north to Kansas railhead towns.

CHAPTER ELEVEN

An Expedition in the Name of Science
· 1841 ·

Early on the morning of April 28, 1841, the *U.S.S. Vincennes*, a seven-hundred-ton sloop of war, approached the craggy Pacific Coast near the mouth of the Columbia River. On board was the U.S. Exploring Expedition, a group appointed by the government in 1838 to gather scientific data from around the world. Its current mission was to explore the shorelines of today's states of Oregon, Washington, and California.

The expedition, under the command of Lieutenant Charles Wilkes, represented the first attempt by the United States to combine the talents of civilian scientists and Navy support personnel. Although the forty-year-old Wilkes had less experience at sea than many other officers, he had been selected, according to one historian, because "he had the vision, intelligence, and determination to do the job." Under his leadership, the explorers succeeded in surveying literally every corner of the globe and collecting tens of thousands of specimens which eventually served as the foundation of the Smithsonian Institution's Museum of Natural History.

From the mouth of the Columbia, the *Vincennes* made its way up the coast, reaching Fort Nisqually, a Hudson's Bay Company post at the south end of Puget Sound, on May 11. There, Wilkes left his ship for a month-long exploration of the interior. He instructed Lieutenant Robert E. Johnson to explore the Cascade Mountains.

Wilkes's own scientific investigation carried him to Fort Vancouver. From there, he sent parties to reconnoiter the

Willamette River Valley, and he personally visited several American settlers there in June. He was impressed by their strong desire to become independent of the British-controlled Hudson's Bay Company. He wrote that

> people were quite alive on the subject of laws, courts, and magistrates, including governors, judges, etc. I was here informed that a committee had been appointed to wait upon mc on my arrival... to hold a consultation relative to the founding of settled governments.

Wilkes advised area residents to bide their time before pushing for admittance to the United States.

Although the official mission of the Exploring Expedition was purely scientific, Wilkes also gathered geographic information that would prove extremely valuable in years to come, when U.S. authorities negotiated with Great Britain over the boundary between Canada and Oregon Territory.

Although the Wilkes expedition was considered a great success, it was not without its problems. In July, one of the explorers' other ships, the *Peacock*, ran aground off Cape Disappointment and was destroyed, along with all the specimens and notes on board. Wilkes was impressed by the hospitality shown by the Hudson's Bay Company during this crisis. It provided the men with food and shelter at Fort Vancouver until another ship could be purchased and outfitted.

Its mission in the Pacific Northwest accomplished, the U.S. Exploring Expedition sailed to New York via San Francisco, the Hawaiian Islands, the Philippines, Singapore, and the Cape of Good Hope. It brought with it hundreds of new species of plants and animals, as well as maps of heretofore unknown regions of the globe. Members had charted almost three hundred Pacific Islands and had determined that the continent of Antarctica was surrounded by sea. Last but not least, they had explored the coastline of the Pacific Northwest as it had never been explored before.

CHAPTER TWELVE

The Great Migration
· 1843 ·

On a fine autumn day in the late 1830s, Philip Leget Edwards, a young Missouri man, surveyed the beautiful Willamette River Valley from his vantage point in the mountains. For nine months, he had endured remarkable hardships, toiling across the Great Plains and the Rocky Mountains before arriving in Oregon. Now, as the birds sang and flitted about him, he enjoyed this paradise at the end of his long trail.

A small spiral of smoke to the north signaled the location of the Methodist mission built a few years earlier by the Reverend Jason Lee. And there were a few scattered farms belonging to other Americans who had already made their homes here. Solomon Smith and Calvin Tibbs were among the first whites to settle in Oregon, in 1832. By now, about two hundred others resided in the valley.

Several years later, Edwards wrote of his emotions that day as he viewed the valley he described as "picturesque and lovely beyond anything to which we of the Mississippi valley have ever been accustomed." In a letter to a friend who had inquired about conditions in Oregon, Edwards wrote in the poetic language of the day,

> Never shall I forget the wild ecstasy of one hour in that Territory.... I thought of the green phantomland beyond, whither retires the spirit of the fierce warrior when the conflict of life is over—and there was intensity of contrast! Below my feet was all that was soft, and bland, and holy—and beyond, all was the stern rivalry of sublimity and grandeur!—and I thought too, of the vast Infinite that made them all! I know not how long I paused—I started at the admonition of my solitary Indian guide, brushed away the unconscious tear from my eye, and rushed down the dark glen before me—the scene of enchantment was gone—but the recollection never!

By the early 1840s, Oregon was on the minds of thousands of Americans intent on making the long trip west and beginning a new life in this place so gloriously described by Edwards and other visitors. Already, the two-thousand-mile-long Oregon Trail had been blazed. In 1843, the largest party of settlers to date set out overland to the Pacific Northwest. Their journey would become known as the Great Migration.

Peter Burnett, a Tennessee-born, Missouri-raised lawyer who later was elected the first American governor of California, was the leader of this massive movement. In later years, he would identify the force that drove him—and no doubt many other settlers—to Oregon. "I saw that a great American community would grow up, in the space of a few years, upon the shores of the distant Pacific," he wrote, "and I felt an ardent desire to aid in this most important enterprise."

Burnett's wagon train to Oregon was typical of those that followed in the next several years. When the party left Independence, Missouri, on May 22, 1843, it comprised nearly three hundred men, women, and children, along with fifty wagons. By the time the train reached the neighborhood of today's city of Topeka, Kansas, these numbers had more than doubled. One hundred and forty-seven days and almost seventeen hundred miles after setting out, Burnett's party reached Fort Walla Walla. Part of the group floated down the Columbia River to Fort Vancouver, while the rest traveled overland to The Dalles and then switched to boats for the final leg of the trip.

Burnett's group, as well as many that followed, found a friend in Dr. John McLoughlin, chief factor of the Hudson's Bay Company post at Fort Vancouver. Prices for commodities were high in Oregon. Burnett wrote that

> pork was ten and flour four cents a pound, and other provisions in proportion. These were high prices considering our scanty means and extra appetites. Had it not been for the generous kindness of the gentlemen in charge of the business of the Hudson's Bay Company, we should have suffered much greater privations.

Burnett estimated that the arrival of his wagon train doubled the population of Oregon. And that was only the beginning. By the time the Civil War broke out in the East, more than a quarter of a million emigrants had left home to seek their fortunes at the end of the Oregon Trail.

By 1848, Oregon had grown so much that it was officially designated a territory. In 1859, it became the nation's thirty-third state.

CHAPTER THIRTEEN

John C. Fremont's Ramble through Oregon
· 1843 ·

O n October 11, 1843, the noted explorer John C. Fremont crossed the imaginary line that today separates Oregon and Idaho. With him on this, his second expedition to the Far West, were his topographer, Charles Preuss; his guide, famed mountain man Thomas Fitzpatrick; Christopher "Kit" Carson; and seventeen other Creole, French-Canadian, and American adventurers. The party had left Missouri on May 17, crossed the Great Plains and the Rocky Mountains, visited the Great Salt Lake, and moved north to Fort Boise before finally crossing into Oregon country.

Fremont was the son-in-law of Senator Thomas Hart Benton of Missouri, a dynamic proponent of westward expansion. The year before, the explorer had followed the route of the future Oregon Trail up the Platte River to the Continental Divide before returning to Missouri and preparing for this much longer expedition of 1843-1844.

In his journal, Fremont described that autumn day in 1843 when he crossed into what is now Oregon:

> The morning was clear, with a light breeze from the east, and a temperature at sunrise of 33 degrees. A part of a bullock purchased at the fort, together with the boat to assist him in crossing, was left here for Mr. Fitzpatrick, and at 11 o'clock we resumed our jour-

ney.... About sunset we reached the Riviere aux Malheurs [the Malheur River], a considerable stream, with an average breadth of 50 feet, and, at this time, 18 inches depth of water.

The following day, Fremont discovered some hot springs and wrote of the event in his journal:

My attention was attracted by a smoke on the right side of the river, a little below the ford, where I found on the low bank, near the water, a considerable number of hot springs, in which the temperature of the water was 193 degrees. The ground, which was too hot for the naked foot, was covered above and below the springs with an incrustation of common salt, very white and good, and fine grained.

Following about the same route that employees of John Jacob Astor's Pacific Fur Company had taken more than thirty years earlier, Fremont and his party reached what is now the Oregon-Washington border in late October. As he neared the Walla Walla River, he spied Mount Hood "standing high out above the surrounding country, at the distance of 180 miles."

On October 24, Fremont's party reached the mission of Marcus and Narcissa Whitman, about thirty miles east of Fort Walla Walla. Whitman was away at the time, but Fremont recorded in his journal that he "had the pleasure to see a fine-looking large family of emigrants, men, women, and children, in robust health."

The next day, the explorers arrived at Fort Walla Walla, a Hudson's Bay Company fur post located at the junction of the Walla Walla and Columbia rivers. Fremont was awed by the Columbia. He wrote:

We here saw, for the first time, the great river on which the course of events for the last half century has been directing attention and conferring historical fame. The river is, indeed, a noble object, and has here attained its full magnitude.

The expedition left Fort Walla Walla on October 28 and followed the Columbia back into Oregon, eventually reaching The Dalles. There, Fremont wrote, "our land journey found... its western termination."

Before turning around to head home, however, Fremont borrowed an Indian canoe and floated downriver to Fort Vancouver, where he intended to purchase supplies for the return trip to Missouri. When he reached the fort a couple of days later, he was met by Dr. John McLoughlin, "who received me with the courtesy and hospitality for which he has been eminently distinguished, and which makes a forcible and delightful impression on a traveller from the long wilderness from which we had issued." Fremont left with his supplies on November 10 and directed his party back up the Columbia to The Dalles.

On November 25, the expedition left the banks of the Columbia behind, intending to head for home. But along the way the men changed their minds. Instead of traveling southeast to the headwaters of the Arkansas River and then east to Missouri as planned, they wandered all over the Great Basin, across the Sierra Nevada to Sutter's Fort in California, through the desert wastelands of the extreme Southwest, and finally, by a circuitous route, across the Rockies and the southern Great Plains. Fremont finally reached St. Louis on August 6, 1844. In the course of his two expeditions, he had mapped much of the country between Missouri and Fort Vancouver, thus paving the way for others to follow.

CHAPTER FOURTEEN

The Founding of Portland
· 1843 ·

It was a bleak winter day in 1843 when two white men and their four Indian companions left Fort Vancouver and floated down the Columbia toward the mouth of the Willamette River. At the confluence, the men steered their canoe up the latter, smaller stream, and headed for Oregon City, a tiny settlement several miles upriver.

One of the men was ill and lay covered in blankets on the floor of the canoe. A transplanted Tennessean, William P. Overton had worked at a Methodist mission at The Dalles before moving to Oregon City. He had made this trip to Fort Vancouver to seek the advice of Dr. John McLoughlin, administrator of the

Hudson's Bay Company fur post. The good-hearted doctor was often called upon to minister to the sick of the region. After treating Overton, McLoughlin asked the other white man, A.L. Lovejoy, a Hudson's Bay Company agent stationed in Oregon City, to return the sick man to his home on the Willamette.

As the canoe sliced through a cold drizzle, Overton began to feel better. He sat up and initiated a conversation with Lovejoy. Once, he said, he had considered starting a new settlement on land he owned on the west bank of the Willamette near its juncture with the Columbia. Now he was having second thoughts. According to Lovejoy's memoirs, Overton told him,

> I am going away. I am going to Texas. I have got enough of this country and if you want a claim, I will give you the best claim there is around here.

Overton suggested that they stop and look at the property. So Lovejoy instructed the Indians to pull the canoe up to the west bank of the Willamette, and he and Overton got out and walked through the dense forest there. Liking what he saw, Lovejoy told Overton, "Very well, sir, I will take it."

Later, Overton decided not to go to Texas after all and asked Lovejoy to return half the claim. Lovejoy recalled,

> I told him I did not consider it worth anything, much. We had not done anything on it.... When he said he wanted half of it back he said: "Let us take it together; we'll go on and improve." "Well," says I, "I will do that; I do not care." I was doing business up here in town [Oregon City] where there was a great share of writing to be done, contracts for logging, etc. He went down there and went to cutting logs and preparing to build a house. He worked nearly the whole winter.

By the spring of 1844, Overton had once again changed his mind, declaring that he would move after all. But when Lovejoy suggested that Overton relinquish his half of the property, the Tennessean refused. He offered to sell it to Lovejoy for one hundred dollars, and when Lovejoy declined, Overton sold it for two hundred to Francis W. Pettygrove, a merchant in Oregon City.

Lovejoy and Pettygrove hired a workman to build a log cabin at what is now the southwest corner of Front and Washington streets. Lovejoy later described this first house in Portland as "nothing but an old log house, and the mosquitos were so thick that the fellow said he could not work... It was full of fleas."

After laying out the new town in the spring of 1845, Lovejoy and Pettygrove debated what to name it. Lovejoy was originally from Boston and Pettygrove from Portland, Maine, and both men wanted to name the settlement after their hometowns. They decided to flip a coin. Pettygrove won.

In the meantime, James B. Stephens, known locally as "Uncle Jimmy," had purchased some land across the Willamette. In 1870, it would be incorporated as East Portland, but it would not prove as attractive to settlers as its sister city. That same year, Portland would boast 8,293 residents, while East Portland was home to only 830.

Lovejoy eventually sold his share of Portland to Benjamin Stark, and Pettygrove sold his half to Daniel H. Lownsdale. Lovejoy became a member of the Oregon provisional legislature in 1848 and later served in the territorial government. "Uncle Jimmy" continued to support the expansion of East Portland until his death in 1889. Some of these pioneers are remembered today by downtown Portland streets named in their honor.

CHAPTER FIFTEEN

Making Headlines Oregon-Style
· 1846 ·

On a cold Thursday in February 1846, W.G. T'Vault left his office in Oregon City carrying a sizable stack of newspapers—the first ever published on the West Coast. Formerly a lawyer, T'Vault had forsaken the profession to edit the newly founded *Oregon Spectator* for three hundred dollars a year. He was also president of the Oregon Printing Association, publisher of the bimonthly paper.

Oregon City had been home to an earlier newspaper of sorts, the colorful *Flumgudgeon Gazette and Bumble Bee Budget*. Handwritten, it had mostly spoofed local citizens and events rather than reported hard news. Consequently, the *Spectator* is recognized not only as Oregon's first newspaper, but as the first on the entire west coast of the United States. It predated the first paper in California by six months and the first in Washington by six and a half years. In fact, among western states, only New Mexico, Oklahoma, and Texas beat Oregon to the printing press.

The first issue of the *Spectator* was a single sheet of paper measuring eleven and a half by seventeen inches, folded down the middle to create four pages. It was printed on a hand press that the Oregon Printing Association had ordered from New York. In addition to carrying the text of the Organic Laws of Oregon, which had been proposed by the Legislative Committee of Oregon Territory, the premier issue contained tidbits of homey advice such as the following, printed on page one.

Be honest, frugal, plain—seek content and happiness at home—be industrious and persevering; and our word for it, if you are in debt you will soon get out of it; if your circumstances are now embarrassed, they will soon become easy, no matter who may be the editor, or what may be the price of flour.

Oregon's second newspaper, the Oregon City *Free Press*, debuted on April 8, 1848. Its editor was George L. Curry, a former editor of the *Spectator* and future governor of the state.

News of the California gold rush had a deleterious effect on both the fledgling *Free Press* and the elder *Spectator*. Both had to suspend publication temporarily for reasons later explained in an apologetic editorial.

The *Spectator* after a temporary sickness greets its patrons and hopes to serve them faithfully.... That "gold fever" which has swept about 3,000 of the officers, lawyers, physicians, farmers, and mechanics of Oregon into the mines of California, took away our printer also.

A unique feature of early Oregon newspapers was their acrimonious "Oregon style" of reporting. According to Robert F. Karolevitz, author of *Newspapering in the Old West*, the so-called Oregon style was the "forerunner of a free-swinging brand of personal journalism" laced with "vituperative, no-holds-barred editorials."

By the mid-1850s, Oregon boasted three prominent newspapers, all of whose editors were masters of Oregon-style reporting. Thomas Jefferson Dryer of Portland's *Weekly Oregonian*, Asahel Bush of Salem's *Oregon Statesman*, and W.L. Adams of the *Oregon Argus* (the successor to the *Spectator* in Oregon City) all used the pages of their newspapers to denounce each other's politics with, as Karolevitz put it, "a seething cauldron of editorial invective which left their readers gasping."

On one occasion Bush, a Democrat, responded to a printed attack by Dryer, a Whig, by refusing to "get down to the depths he has sunk to... for we will not sully our columns with vulgarity and slang." Later, the outraged Bush added:

> There is not a brothel in the land that would not have felt itself disgraced by the presence of the *Oregonian* of week before last. It was a complete tissue of gross profanity, obscenity, falsehood, and meanness. And yet it was but little below the standard of that characterless sheet.

One by one, newspapers were established in other Oregon towns. By 1867, Eugene had its *Guard* and residents of Roseburg could subscribe to the new *Ensign* for a mere three dollars a year, paid in advance.

Professional journalism had come to Oregon, and as shaky as its early foundations were, it provided the basis upon which state newspapering traditions of today are built.

CHAPTER SIXTEEN

The Birth of the Wool Industry
· 1848 ·

Joseph Watt, a thirty-one-year-old Ohio native who had called Missouri home for the past ten years, did not make a particularly good first impression when he arrived in Oregon City in the summer of 1844. When the wagon train he had been traveling with had come to within three hundred miles of the end of the Oregon Trail, it had fallen on hard times, and Watt and a companion had decided to strike out on their own. With a rifle and a single loaf of bread between them, the pair had headed cross-country. By the time Watt reached Oregon City, his clothes were tattered and filthy.

Soon after his arrival, Watt encountered Dr. John McLoughlin, chief factor of Fort Vancouver. Noted for his kindness to emigrants and other travelers, McLoughlin was shocked at Watt's appearance, and he instructed his clerk to

> give this man some clothes. Tut! Tut! Tut! What people these Americans are. Wandering vagabonds across a continent. What are they coming here for? Give him some clothes.

Watt secured a job as a carpenter in Oregon City and, after paying back McLoughlin for the clothes, he began saving every penny he could. The town already boasted about six hundred residents, and Watt had no trouble staying employed as more and more emigrants arrived every year.

Watt had always been interested in livestock. In fact, he had intended to move to Texas and make his living as a cattle rancher. But when he got as far as Arkansas, he was lured northward by rumors of a paradise in the Pacific Northwest. Now that he was making a decent living, his thoughts again turned to livestock, only this time he had sheep on his mind.

Although sheep had been grazing the Oregon range for quite a few years, it was not until 1844, with the same caravan that Watt had accompanied, that sheep actually traveled cross-country from the East to Oregon. Watt was convinced that the Willamette Valley would make ideal sheep country, so he returned to Missouri in 1847 and gradually purchased a herd of his own, mostly purebred Merinos. In 1848, he and his 435 animals headed west with a caravan that included his parents, seven sisters, and a brother.

Watt managed to get 330 of his sheep safely to Oregon, where he and his father staked large claims in Yamhill County. He turned his sheep loose to graze on his property, little knowing that these animals would provide the basis upon which Oregon's valuable wool industry would build.

The following winter was harsh, and Watt lost much of his stock. Nonetheless, he harvested enough wool to knit 150 pairs of socks, which he sold for three to four dollars a pair. In 1849, he traveled to California to sell his wares to the gold miners and was struck by the great demand for woolen garments. All that was needed was a woolen mill to convert the raw wool into cloth.

For the next several years, Watt planned and saved, and in 1857 he opened the Willamette Woolen Manufacturing Company in Salem, the first woolen mill in Oregon. A guest at the grand opening of the mill described it as "an immense pile of buildings 7 stories high, containing 381 large windows, in each of which was placed 32 large candles, the effect of which, when lighted, was bright indeed." Local girls were hired to operate the nearly five hundred spindles and eleven looms.

The first blankets made at Watt's mill sold for between twenty-five and seventy-five dollars each. They and the flannel cloth that soon followed were the first in a long line of superior Oregon woolen products. Today, the state ranks as one of the top producers in the nation of wool blankets and garments.

CHAPTER SEVENTEEN

Joe Meek's Momentous Missions
· 1849 ·

Joe Meek was a man in a hurry. He had spent several weeks convincing officials in Washington, D.C., that Oregon deserved to be a U.S. territory, and he had watched with satisfaction as President James K. Polk authorized the request on August 14, 1848. Now Meek, newly appointed U.S. marshal for the fledgling territory, was headed home.

Not surprisingly, Polk wanted the credit for Oregon's elevated status. He asked Meek, a distant relative, to deliver the good news to Oregonians before his term as president expired on March 3. So Meek set out across the continent with all haste.

Stopping to pick up the newly appointed territorial governor, General Joseph Lane of Indiana, along the way, Meek hurried from Washington to St. Louis, followed the Santa Fe Trail to New Mexico, and took a wagon road across the desert to California. In San Francisco, the two men boarded the ship *Jeanette* and sailed up the Pacific Coast to the mouth of the Columbia River.

By now it was March, and time was running out. Meek and Lane took a smaller craft up the Columbia and Willamette rivers to Oregon City, the provisional capital. Incredibly, they arrived on March 2, with one day to spare!

Lane announced the good news the following day, and Meek relaxed, knowing he had kept his promise to the president.

Meek was a Virginian, but he decided early in life that he wanted to be a mountain man. He wandered the West for more than a decade before settling in the Willamette Valley with his Nez Perce wife.

Meek was a large, fun-loving man. His biographer, Stanley Vestal, described him as

the Davy Crockett of our Great Northwest, bold adventurous, humorous, a first-class trapper, pioneer, peace officer, and frontier politician. More, he was the wittiest, saltiest, most shameless wag and jester that ever wore moccasins in the Rockies—a tall, happy go-lucky Virginian, lover of practical jokes, tall tales, Jacksonian democracy, and Indian women.... Of all... mountain men, none was more typically American than Joe Meek—and none so completely engaging.

Meek served as U.S. marshal for Oregon Territory for four years, no doubt keeping plenty busy trying to maintain peace on the wild frontier. Soon after he began his job, he became involved in a case that meant a great deal to him personally. This was the trial of the Cayuse Indians accused of murdering his friends, Marcus and Narcissa Whitman, on November 29, 1847. A dozen other people had been killed during the incident, and forty-seven had been taken prisoner.

The Whitmans had migrated west eleven years earlier at the request of the American Board of Commissioners for Foreign Missions, a group that represented the Dutch Reformed Lutheran, Presbyterian, and Congregational churches. The couple married shortly before their journey. Narcissa was one of the first white women to cross the Rocky Mountains.

The Whitmans were eager to teach the Indians the benefits of Christianity, and they worked hard at their calling. Their mission, built near what is now Walla Walla, Washington, was soon well-known and respected by the tribes of the Columbia River Valley. When emigrants began flocking westward via the Oregon Trail, the mission became a regular stopover.

Since Whitman was a physician, visitors often solicited his medical skills. On one occasion, he removed an arrowhead from the back of the famed guide and mountain man, Jim Bridger.

No one knows exactly why the Cayuses killed the Whitmans, but their motives appear to be complex. The Indians had recently suffered through a measles epidemic, and perhaps they failed to understand why Whitman, a man of medicine, could not stop their people from dying. White settlers brought with them many other diseases for which the Indians had no immunity. The natives may have wondered why the white people Whitman attended often recovered while many of the Indians, treated for the same diseases, did not. Whatever the reasons, admiration and respect for the Whitmans turned to fear and hate, and the Cayuses fell upon the mission with a deadly purpose.

Five Cayuse warriors were arrested for the murders and brought to Oregon City to stand trial. Meek vividly described the event.

> Captain Claiborne led off for the defence. He foamed and ranted like he were acting a play in some theatre. He knew about as much law as one of the Indians he were defending; and his gestures were so powerful that he smashed two tumblers that the Judge had ordered to be filled with cold water for him.... Mr. Prichett closed for the defence with a very able argument; for he were a man of brains. But then followed Mr. Amory Holbrook, for the prosecution, and he laid down the case so plain that the jury were convinced before they left the jurybox. When the Judge passed sentence of death on them, two of the chief's showed no terror; but the other three were filled with horror and consternation that they could not conceal.

On June 3, 1850, Meek supervised the hanging of the five Indians.

> I brought out the five prisoners and placed them on the drop. Then the chief, Ki-am-sump-kin, who always had declared his innocence, begged me to kill him with my

knife—for an Indian fears to be hanged. But I soon put an end to his entreaties by cutting the rope which held the drop with my tomahawk. As I said, "The Lord have mercy on your souls," the trap fell, and the five Cayuses hung in the air. Three of them died instantly. The other two struggled for several minutes.... After thirty-five minutes they were taken down and buried.

Meek's role in the early development of Oregon cannot be overstated. Whether as lawman, political spokesman, soldier, or just plain citizen, the garrulous mountain man left an indelible mark on the land and its people. When he died in 1875 at his home near Hillsboro, Oregon, old Joe was already a legend. As Vestal put it, "Nobody who knows his story can possibly think of Joe Meek as dead. He was always so magnificently alive!"

CHAPTER EIGHTEEN

The Minting of the Oregon "Beaver"
· 1849 ·

In early 1849, eight men gathered in Oregon City to discuss a situation that was becoming increasingly bothersome—and expensive: The U.S. government had made no effort to establish coin or currency standards in the far-off Pacific Northwest. People still relied on the barter system when they wanted to buy or sell commodities. But swapping goods and services was burdensome and often unfair. Clearly, a better system was needed.

Oregonians had been bartering for years. Early in the state's history, fur companies had relied on trade with the Indians to acquire the valuable pelts that kept them in business. Early settlers had continued to barter with no undue hardships. The problems started when gold was discovered in California in January 1848. Hundreds of Oregonians rushed to the Sacramento area in search of an easy fortune. According to Leslie M. Scott, who wrote about the situation in 1932,

> Oregon very naturally sent a great number of her population together with all the supplies that she could spare from her immediate wants, receiving in return a large amount of gold dust of the most superior quality.

There was no standard in Oregon upon which to base the value of gold, other than that specified by the distant federal government—about eleven dollars an ounce. Worse yet, there were few scales in the region to accurately weigh the gold. As a result, no one really knew how much gold to give or take for the items he was purchasing or selling.

The U.S. Constitution specifically gave the federal government exclusive rights "to coin Money, regulate the Value thereof, and of foreign Coin, and fix the Standard of Weights and Measures." Nonetheless, the Oregon provisional legislature passed a law in February 1849 giving private companies the right to mint territorial money. The meeting in Oregon City was to determine how to go about it.

The eight men who had gathered—W.K. Kilborne, Theophilus Magruder, James Taylor, George Abernethy, W.H. Willson, William H. Rector, John G. Campbell, and Noyes Smith—decided to establish a nonprofit entity called the Oregon Exchange Company to mint gold coinage.

First, the company needed minting equipment. A blacksmith named Thomas Powell was hired to forge the press and other tools, mostly using the iron from old wagon wheels. He was paid a dollar for every pound of iron he used—about sixty dollars by the time he was finished.

The Oregon Exchange Company decided to mint two denominations: five- and ten-dollar gold pieces. The initial of each of the company's founders was stamped on the five-dollar coin, except that Campbell's C was mistakenly printed as G. Abernethy's and Willson's initials were omitted from the ten-dollar piece, which was minted later. Both coins carried the stamped imprint of a beaver, much like the tokens used in Oregon by the North West Company before it was absorbed by the Hudson's Bay Company in 1821. Accordingly, the new coins were called "beavers."

Now that Oregon had its own gold standard, the price per ounce rose from eleven to sixteen dollars. The beavers were also worth eight to ten percent more than federally minted coins because they were made completely of gold and contained no alloys as the U.S. coins did.

In March 1849, the citizens of Oregon learned officially that the region had been designated a territory. When the first territorial governor, Joseph Lane, arrived in the Willamette Valley that month, he declared it illegal for Oregonians to mint their own coinage. Nonetheless, the Oregon Exchange Company stayed in business until September, producing six thousand five-dollar coins and 2,850 ten-dollar pieces.

CHAPTER NINETEEN

The Making of a Poet
· 1852 ·

It was a beautiful fall day in 1852 when Cincinnatus Hiner Miller, an inquisitive, bright-eyed, thirteen-year-old boy, arrived with his family at the headwaters of the Willamette River. Nat, as his family called him, had been born in Indiana. But his father, a Quaker school teacher, had moved his family to Illinois before deciding to follow the Oregon Trail westward in search of a new beginning.

Although the long journey across the continent was grueling and perilous, Nat enjoyed it thoroughly. Already an adventuresome lad, he had heard of the explorer John C. Fremont, and now he followed in the very footsteps of the man known as the Great Pathfinder.

The Millers settled first on the Santiam River and later filed a claim for 320 acres farther south on the McKenzie River. The land was not well-suited to agriculture, so Nat's father, Hulings, went to work part-time as a school teacher to earn extra money. Nat and his younger brother, James, did most of the farm chores, but, his mother recalled later, "he was a queer little boy who never played, was seldom without a book, and would hastily complete his chores in order to lie back and read while his brother caught up with him."

One of Nat's acquaintances was a pack-train driver named "Mountain Joe" De Bloney, who was a frequent guest at the Millers' remote wilderness cabin. Young Nat listened intently every time Mountain Joe spun a yarn about his adventures and wide-spread travels. The impressionable boy soon yearned to be free of farm life and to set out on his own quest for adventure. When he was fifteen, he took off for the gold-mining camps of southern Oregon and northern California.

After a couple of years as a cook in the filthy, tempestuous mining camps and a brief experiment living with the Digger Indians, the disenchanted Miller returned home, leaving a Digger wife and daughter behind. He returned to school, took the bar exam in Portland, passed, and then decided to forego practicing law. Instead, he established a pony express that for a short time ran between Washington Territory and what was soon to be Idaho Territory.

Still later, Miller purchased a Eugene, Oregon, newspaper, the *Democratic Register*. He adopted the pseudonym "Joaquin" and in 1868 saw publication of his first book of poetry.

Miller's newspaper failed, partly because of his pro-Confederate sympathies in overwhelmingly pro-Union Oregon. In the meantime, he had married again. The young woman, Minnie Dyer, had been entranced by his poetry, but in only a few years she became disillusioned and left with their two children. During that time, Miller was elected to a judgeship in Grant County.

Two volumes of poetry later, Miller traveled to California, where he soon found himself rubbing elbows with such literary giants as Bret Harte. Convinced now of his own literary success, he began calling himself "the Byron of the Rockies."

Miller moved on to England, where he was thrilled to walk the ground once trod by Lord Byron and Robert Burns. Most of his poetry found fair acceptance in Europe but created little stir in the United States. Pained by his countrymen's disinterest, Miller spent the next several years traveling through South America and Europe. When he finally returned to the United States, he lived briefly in New York, Boston, and Washington, D.C., before establishing a home in Oakland, California, with a third wife. There, he built his estate, "The Heights," complete with gardens and shrines to his literary heroes.

Thirteen years after Miller's death, Stanley Thomas Williams tried to describe the unconventional poet in his 1926 book, *The American Spirit in Letters*.

He had won the admiration of various distinguished men of his time, though some of these were inclined to smile, as did Bret Harte in the early days, at this compound of madness and poetic genius. For in this conventional world of ours the performance of the Sierra poet was distinctly anomalous. He was one of the most original writers America has produced, but he was also a slavish imitator of Byron and Swinburne. He was a child of the plains, yet he bore himself in society like a Spanish grandee. He wrote some poetry as sublime as the Canadian Rockies, yet sixty per cent of his production was rubbish.

Miller remained eccentric to the end. On his death bed, when his physician urged him to take his medication, he replied, "Doctor, I am a poet. It is not poetic to take pills." His final request was to be cremated atop a large funeral pyre that he had built on his estate in Oakland. When city officials pointed out that cremation of a human body within the city limits was illegal, his large circle of friends had to content themselves with casting the ashes of his legally cremated body onto the burning pyre.

CHAPTER TWENTY

Louis Remme's Remarkable Ride
• 1855 •

Monday, February 26, 1855, was a day that Louis Remme would never forget. Sliding off his exhausted horse at Stewart's Livery in Portland, he breathlessly asked the attendant if the ship from San Francisco had arrived. When the boy said no, the French-Canadian cattle dealer asked for directions to the Adams & Company bank. He sped off almost before the lad had finished his explanation.

Tired and haggard, Remme hastened down one of Portland's main streets, acutely aware of the strange looks he was getting. He did not care whether he was dirty and smelly. What was important was that he reach the Portland branch office of the Adams & Company bank before the ship from San Francisco docked at the wharf with the latest news from California.

At the bank, Remme spied a nattily dressed gentlemen whom he assumed to be the manager and presented him with a certificate of deposit. He pointed out that the certificate had been issued by the Sacramento branch of Adams & Company, and he asked the manager to cash it. The manager agreed to do so for a service fee of half of one percent. Then he went to the vault and returned with $12,437.50.

Thanking the man profusely, Remme placed the money in a cloth sack. He bolted out the door, hurried to a hotel, rented a room, and instructed the desk clerk to place the bag of money in the hotel safe.

Remme did not even take time to clean up before retracing his steps to the bank. With a wicked smile, he advised the bank manager to "save" himself. The flustered man eyed his disheveled customer and asked for an explanation. Remme explained that Adams & Company had failed and that all of the bank's properties in California had been attached.

The bank manager refused to believe it. Adams & Company was one of the soundest and most trustworthy financial institutions on the West Coast.

"You'll find I'm right when the steamer gets in," Remme told him.

Even as the two men talked, a cannon signaled the arrival of the ship *Columbia* at the Portland wharf. Within minutes, a constable entered the bank and served a writ of attachment on the manager at the request of Ralph Meade, purser of the *Columbia*, who had $950 on deposit there. The bewildered manager walked to the door and hesitatingly placed a "Closed" sign on it as Remme headed back to his hotel.

After he had bathed, shaved, and eaten a long-overdue meal, Remme sat in the hotel dining room and reflected on the difficult week he had just endured. Only seven days ago, he had been in San Francisco, celebrating his good fortune at concluding a particularly rewarding business transaction. The result of the deal was $12,500 in gold, which Remme promptly deposited in the Sacramento branch of Adams & Company.

While he was wining and dining in San Francisco, he heard some alarming news. The largest financial company west of the Allegheny Mountains—the firm of Page, Bacon & Company of St. Louis—had just failed. Since Page, Bacon had just opened a branch in San Francisco, the news naturally caused panic among the bank's depositors. An immediate run depleted the bank of most of its cash. Fearing other failures, desperate depositors withdrew their funds from other banks as well, including Adams & Company, the bank that held Remme's $12,500.

Remme hurried to Sacramento and was standing in line at the Adams & Company's local branch when it opened for business on February 20. The bank had liquidated, and no deposits were being refunded. A miserable Remme was wondering what to do next when it occurred to him that Adams & Company had a branch bank in Portland. If he could get there before news of the bank failure, he might be able to get his money back! It was a wild idea, but it was worth a try.

Remme took a boat from Sacramento to Knight's Landing, about forty miles to the north. There, he acquired a horse and spurred it northward through the Sacramento Valley, stopping for nothing except the purchase of fresh horses and a little sleep and nourishment. Remme rode day and night until he reached the Oregon border, more than a seventy-hour ride from Sacramento. Soon after he crossed into Oregon, he was attacked by Indians, but luckily he escaped.

On and on Remme rode, until he reached Oregon City. He had hoped to board a steamboat there but was disappointed to find that none would go downriver to Portland until the following day. Mounting again, Remme rode on until he reached Stewart's Livery in Portland around noon on February 26.

Remarkably, Remme had ridden 665 miles in only 143 hours, including ten hours of sleep and very brief stops for food. He had essentially earned eighty-seven dollars an hour, or nineteen dollars a mile. The alternative would have been to lose all his money.

As he left his Portland hotel to arrange his return to California, Remme decided that the trip had been well worth the effort.

CHAPTER TWENTY-ONE

A Monopoly on the Columbia
· 1860 ·

During a meeting of the board of directors of the Oregon Steam Navigation Company, probably sometime in the early 1870s, Captain T.W. Lyles of San Francisco, a major stockholder, slowly rose from his chair and asked to be heard. The board had concluded its business, so the chairman recognized Lyles. With a somber look on his face, the captain proceeded to speak.

Mr. Chairman, I move that Eph Day, a purser on one of our boats, be discharged from the service of the company. I see, gentlemen, that Eph Day is purser on a boat of only 150 tons register, yet I find that he comes in at the end of every trip with a report of having carried from 250 to 300 tons of freight, and, gentlemen, he substantiates his reports by bringing in the cash for those amounts of freight. Now, while I do not claim to be much of a steamboat man, yet I can see, gentlemen, that if we allow our boats to be overladen in this manner and made to carry twice as much as they were designed to carry, they will soon be worn out and we will have no boats.

Everyone in the room howled when they realized the captain was speaking facetiously, that he was actually proud of the company's ability to deliver more freight up and down the Columbia River than its steamboats were built to carry. In fact, the captain's words underscored the shrewd and hard-nosed business principles that had made the company so successful.

The Oregon Steam Navigation Company was incorporated in late December 1860. It had twenty-five stockholders and two million dollars in capital. Stock sold for five hundred dollars a share.

Although commercial traffic on the Columbia had existed for a number of years, the Oregon Steam Navigation Company was the first to consolidate several operations under one roof and to offer complete transportation facilities from Portland all the way to Lewiston, Idaho Territory. In providing this badly needed service to a rapidly expanding population, the company had managed to monopolize navigation on the Columbia. The consumer either paid the company's exorbitant prices—for example, forty dollars a ton to ship freight the one hundred miles between Portland and The Dalles—or his goods sat on the dock. Passage from Portland to The Dalles was eight dollars, plus seventy-five cents extra for meals. Passage from Portland to Lewiston was sixty dollars, plus a dollar a bed. This was at a time when a night's lodging in a good hotel cost fifty cents and a decent dinner could be had for a quarter.

P.W. Gillette wrote of the company's price-gouging in 1904:

So enormous were the charges for freight and passage,
I am credibly informed, that the steamer *Okanogan*
paid the entire cost of herself on her first trip. It makes
my head swim now, as memory carries me back to
those wonderfully rushing days, when the constant fall
of chinking coin into the coffers of the company was
almost like the flow of a dashing torrent. The Oregon
Steam Navigation Company had become a millionaire-
making machine.

As the Oregon Steam Navigation Company approached its
twentieth anniversary, a story appeared in the Portland newspapers that caused consternation among the stockholders and
directors. According to the article, Jay Gould, the famed New York
financier, was about to extend his railroad to the Pacific Coast. He
also planned to begin offering steamship service along the
Columbia River, the story said. It appeared that the company was
about to get some serious competition. No longer would it be able
to charge those outrageous prices.

Shortly after the appearance of the Jay Gould article, the
Oregon Steam Navigation Company sold out to Henry Villard, a
German immigrant who had done well since coming to America
in 1853. Villard, already well-known in railroad circles, paid five
million dollars for the company and quickly reorganized it into
the Oregon Railway and Navigation Company. He constructed a
railroad from Portland eastward along the Oregon bank of the
Columbia River. According to Gillette, the new company soon
reduced its rates, giving farmers the incentive to increase production and thus stimulating the economy.

After the sale, a rumor circulated that the Jay Gould article
had been a hoax, possibly arranged by Villard, to frighten the
company's owners into selling. True or not, the artificially high
fares of the old Oregon Steam Navigation Company were a thing
of the past.

CHAPTER TWENTY-TWO

A Journey up the Columbia
· 1865 ·

In 1865, five distinguished gentlemen boarded a steamer in Portland and began a two-day excursion up the Columbia River. Despite the July heat, they wore their finest black suits, white shirts with stiff collars, and stylish top hats. Their names may well have been familiar to some of their fellow passengers. They were Schuyler Colfax, speaker of the U.S. House of Representatives; Samuel Bowles, editor of the Springfield, Massachusetts, *Republican*; William Bross, lieutenant governor of Illinois; Albert D. Richardson, a correspondent for the New York *Tribune*; and George K. Otis, an agent with the Overland Stage Line in New York.

This river voyage was part of a two-month "summer's journey" of the American West that the men had undertaken. The steamer, which Bowles described as "capacious and comfortable as the best of those on eastern rivers," soon passed the site of Fort Vancouver. The fort, Bowles later wrote, was

a famous spot in this valley, first as a leading station of the Hudson Bay Company for many years, and since and now as the chief military station of the United States in the interior North-west. Here many of our prominent military men have served apprenticeship,—Grant, Hooker, McClellan and Ingles among them. They are all well remembered in the days of their captaincies here by the old inhabitants.

A little farther up the river, the men spied Mount Hood looming high above the thick evergreen forests to the south. "This is the great snow peak of Oregon," exclaimed Bowles, "its Shasta, its Rainier, its Mount Blanc." After a few more miles, the steamer approached the Cascades, a length of severe rapids that would be tamed seventy years later by the giant Bonneville Dam. There, the passengers were transferred to a train that carried them for five miles around the rapids.

Bowles and his friends were not alone in their awe of the Cascades. Captains Meriwether Lewis and William Clark had approached the rapids in late October 1805 and had described them thus:

> This Great Shute or falls is about 1/2 a mile with the water of this great river Compressed within the Space of 150 paces in which there is great numbers of both large and Small rocks, water passing with great velocity forming & boiling in a most horriable manner, with a fall of about 20 feet, below it widens to about 200 paces and current gentle for a Short distance.

The Bowles party traveled the forty-five or so miles from the Cascades to The Dalles aboard a second "large and equally luxurious" steamboat. Bowles's description of this stretch of the Columbia is pure poetry:

> The dark, basaltic stones lie along in even layers, seamed as in the walls of human structure; then they change to upright form, and run up in well-rounded columns, one after another, one above another. Often is rich similitude to ruined castles of the Rhine; more frequently, fashions and forms, too massive, too majestic, too unique for human ambition and art to aspire to.

At The Dalles, the party circumvented another set of rapids by train. Boarding yet another steamer "with every appointment of comfort and luxury that are found in the best of eastern river craft," Bowles and his friends continued on to the small town of Celilo, where they turned around for the return trip. They had traveled 260 miles one way, and still, according to the incredulous Bowles, the river was navigable by large boats for at least another 160 miles.

Bowles found Portland to be a delightful city. It had become so popular with easterners that property sold for an astounding four hundred dollars a front foot! The population had reached about seven thousand souls, most of whom attended Methodist, Presbyterian, or Catholic churches. The newspaper had a daily circulation of 2,500, or more than a third of the total population—an excellent accomplishment by today's standards. All in all, Bowles thought, Portland had "the air and the fact of a prosperous, energetic town, with a good deal of eastern leadership and tone to business and society and morals."

From Portland, the Bowles party departed for what is now the state of Washington. In the course of their tour, the men also visited Colorado, California, Nevada, and Utah. They traveled "some twelve thousand miles, half by sea, nearly a third by stage, and the balance by railroad and river."

In Bowles's opinion, nothing compared with the beauty of Oregon.

> I was prepared for California. But Oregon is more of a revelation. It has rarer natural beauties, richer resources, a larger development, and a more promising future.... We were told that to see Oregon we must take another week of day and night stage riding.... But no week's riding has given us greater or richer variety of experience; more beauty of landscape; more revelation of knowledge; more pleasure and less pain.

After returning home, Bowles wrote a book about his experiences in the West. Published in 1865, it was entitled *Across the Continent: A Summer's Journey to the Rocky Mountains, the*

Mormons, and the Pacific States, with Speaker Colfax. Richardson, the *Tribune* correspondent, also wrote a book. His *Beyond the Mississippi* was published in 1867. As for Colfax, he went on to become vice president of the United States under Ulysses S. Grant.

CHAPTER TWENTY-THREE

The Execution of Captain Jack
· 1873 ·

The four prisoners at Fort Klamath sat on the edge of their narrow bunks and listened to the pounding of hammers and the shouts of men—the sounds of a gallows being erected outside their gloomy cell. They knew this bitter day in October 1873 was going to be their last.

The condemned men were Modoc Indians named Captain Jack, Boston Charley, Black Jim, and Schonchin John. They were the leaders of a recent uprising that had culminated in the murder of a U.S. brigadier general. Like many Indian revolts during the late nineteenth century, this one had been precipitated by a government attempt to move the Modoc tribe out of its traditional homeland and onto a reservation.

At first, Jack and several other Modoc leaders had agreed to share a reservation with their enemies, the Klamath Indians. They had even signed a treaty to that effect. But the arrangement did not work out. After a year of intolerable conditions on the reservation near Upper Klamath Lake, Jack and a few followers left the agency and resettled on their traditional lands along the Lost River, southeast of today's town of Klamath Falls.

For seven years, the Modocs maintained an uneasy peace with the American settlers who had immigrated to the valley. But as the white population increased and good land became harder to find, the Bureau of Indian Affairs decided to enforce the old treaty. In November 1872, Captain James Jackson was dispatched from Fort Klamath with a troop of cavalry. His orders were to persuade the Modocs to return to the Klamath Reservation.

Jackson's confrontation with Captain Jack was brief and violent. When the gunsmoke cleared, one soldier and eight Indians were dead. Seven other troopers lay wounded. Jack and his followers headed south and holed up in the arid lava beds that surrounded Lake Tule, just across the California border. There, in the wasteland the local Indians called the "land of burnt-out fires," Jack decided to make his last stand.

To mount its offensive against the renegade Modocs, the Army chose Brigadier General Edward R.S. Canby, a fifty-five-year-old veteran of the Seminole, Mexican, and Civil wars. Although Canby sympathized with the Indians, he wasted no time in sending his troops to dislodge them from the lava beds. In the next two months, several soldiers and Modocs died in skirmishes that failed at flushing Captain Jack from his craggy stronghold. Finally, in March 1873, Canby personally took charge of the offensive.

Canby arranged a meeting with Jack and a few of his chieftains on April 11—Good Friday. The meeting was a disaster. Captain Jack drew a pistol and shot Canby at point-blank range, then finished the job with his knife. When Canby's dead body slumped to the floor of the tent, Jack stripped the general of his jacket and put it on amid the shouts of his followers. There was no turning back now. The Modocs fled back to the lava beds, more determined than ever to die fighting.

The stand-off continued until June 1, when Captain Jack, exhausted and dejected, surrendered to the Army. Along with three other leaders of the rebellion, he was taken to Fort Klamath to stand trial. As expected, the Modocs were sentenced to hang.

It was a cold day, October 3, 1873, when a contingent of army guards led Captain Jack, Boston Charley, Black Jim, and Schonchin John out of the stockade. The condemned men were positioned over the trap doors in the floor of the gallows, and their heads were draped with black hoods. As the crowd watched and cheered, the doors sprang open, and the Modocs dropped to their deaths.

Soldiers buried the four Indians at Fort Klamath, but Captain Jack's body was later exhumed and sent to Washington, D.C., where it reportedly became a side-show exhibit. Eventually, the body was presented to the Smithsonian Institution, where it was displayed as an example of Indian anatomy.

It had taken one thousand soldiers and a half million dollars to subdue Captain Jack and end the Modoc War of 1872-1873.

CHAPTER TWENTY-FOUR

The Bannock War
· 1878 ·

Captain Reuben Frank Bernard was tired. For the past couple of weeks, he and his four troops of cavalry had been chasing a sizable band of Bannock Indians from the Camas Prairie in Idaho through the bleak, arid country of southeastern Oregon. On June 22, 1878, the soldiers were camped near Silver Creek, west of Harney Lake.

The next morning, Bernard studied the Bannock camp through his binoculars. He estimated that it held maybe eight hundred men, women, and children. He and his men were badly outnumbered.

Bernard was no novice Indian fighter. The forty-two-year-old Tennessean had spent many years in the Southwest, chasing the Apaches and their legendary leader, Cochise. He had seen limited action back east during the Civil War and had then transferred to California to help fight the Modocs. Now, here he was in Oregon, trying to quell an uprising by Bannocks who resented white encroachment upon their homeland in neighboring Idaho. Because of a careless transcription error by an army clerk several years earlier—he had written "Kansas" instead of "Camas" when defining the Bannock tribal lands—whites were disregarding the treaties signed by the Bannocks and the federal government.

Less than a year earlier, the Army had chased Chief Joseph and his band of Nez Perce out of Oregon and across seventeen hundred miles of Idaho, Wyoming, and Montana wilderness. The Bannocks sleeping in the camp below had been the Army's allies then, serving as scouts in the Nez Perce War.

But in the spring of 1878, Bannock warriors under the

command of Buffalo Horn had shot and wounded three white cattlemen near the Camas Prairie in Idaho. When the men had reported the incident to army authorities, Bernard and his troopers had been dispatched from Fort Boise to join a larger command being assembled by General O.O. Howard.

Now, at a signal from Bernard, the bugler sounded the attack. The four troops of blue-clad cavalry swept down into the valley, shooting and shouting as they rode. They succeeded in surprising the Indians, and within a few minutes most of the Bannock defenders had fled into the rocky bluffs along the creek. Bernard regrouped and attacked again. But this time, his command was repelled by Indians hiding in the rocks. Bernard tried a third charge, but to no avail. Three soldiers and five Indians died in the course of the morning. Two from each side were wounded.

Two weeks later, General Howard himself, accompanied by Bernard and his men, led an attack on the Bannocks several miles south of Pendleton. Howard was afraid the Indians were planning to cross the Columbia River and would spread their havoc in Washington as well. When some Umatilla Indians refused to help the Bannocks cross, a few were murdered out of anger.

Two days later, the Bannocks attacked the stage station on the Pendleton-La Grande road. The next day, some Umatillas, under the guise of helping the Bannocks, invited the Bannock Chief Egan to a parley. The Umatillas murdered Egan, severed his head, and presented it to the Army as proof of their enemy's demise. Without the leadership of Egan and Buffalo Horn, who had been killed in earlier combat, the Bannocks were confounded. They retreated, and so ended the short-lived Bannock War.

CHAPTER TWENTY-FIVE

The Exile of Chief Joseph
·1900·

For Chief Joseph, it was a sentimental journey, this trip into the Wallowa Valley of northeastern Oregon. With an escort of four men, one of them an inspector for the Bureau of Indian Affairs, the sixty-year-old Nez Perce leader was on his way to visit the gravesites of his father and mother.

When Joseph climbed from the buggy to stand beside his father's grave, he must have been reminded of the old man's prophetic words, uttered just before he died in 1871:

A few more years and the white men will be all around you. They have their eyes on this land. My son, never forget my words. This country holds your father's body. Never sell the bones of your father and mother.

Now, reflecting on how many years it had been since the Nez Perce had called the Wallowa home, those words must have pained him.

Joseph's pilgrimage to his parents' graves that summer day marked the second trip he had made to the Wallowa Valley lately. In 1899, he had tried to persuade residents of Enterprise to sell some of their land to the BIA so that the Nez Perce could leave their reservation and return here to their original homeland. The request had fallen on deaf ears, so Joseph had gone to Washington, D.C., to carry his plea to the secretary of the interior. It was this government official who had ordered the BIA inspector to investigate the situation.

To Joseph's sorrow, the inspector recommended that the Nez Perce remain on the Colville Reservation in eastern Washington—their involuntary home since their defeat by Colonel Nelson Miles in 1877. And so it was there, on an early fall day in 1904, that Chief Joseph died. The official cause of death was listed as a massive heart attack, but, according to the reservation doctor, "Joseph died of a broken heart."

Joseph had been born in what is now Idaho, but white settlers in the region had eventually pushed Joseph's people into the Wallowa Valley, where they became known as the Lower Nez Perce. It was not long before settlers coveted the Wallowa, too, so the American government tried to convince the Nez Perce to move farther north.

But the Lower Nez Perce were determined to stay in the beautiful Wallowa Valley. They had not signed earlier treaties between the government and the other Nez Perce bands, so they did not feel bound by any document demanding their removal.

In 1877, General William Tecumseh Sherman, at the request of the U.S. commissioner of Indian affairs, sent troops to enforce a government edict demanding that all non-treaty Indians move to reservations in spite of their protests. Joseph's small band resisted peacefully until June, when a few young warriors, caught up in the emotion of the issue, killed some white settlers. From that point on, in the eyes of the federal government, Joseph and his followers were renegades.

Joseph and his advisors decided to flee the Army, and so, in mid-1877, the Lower Nez Perce began a circuitous journey that would take them more than a thousand miles from home.

Joseph's party crossed into Idaho, fought a couple of engagements along the way, and entered Montana with the objective of eventually reaching Canada and escaping American authority. On August 9, they were confronted by Colonel John Gibbon and a superior Army force in the Big Hole Valley in southwestern Montana. The Nez Perce fought fiercely, and despite eighty-nine casualties, they broke away and continued toward their destination. They dropped southward and eastward, swung through the newly created Yellowstone National Park and headed north.

In the Bears Paw Mountains, Joseph stopped to rest. It was September 29 and beginning to grow cold. His followers were tired, and although the Canadian border was only forty miles away, the Nez Perce decided to make camp for one night.

What Joseph and the others did not know was that Miles and some four hundred troopers, supported by a company of Sioux and Cheyenne scouts and a couple of pieces of artillery, were advancing rapidly. At eight o'clock on the morning of September 30, Miles and his men attacked.

The fighting was fierce. After the initial surprise attack, a second and then a third were directed by Miles. In all three cases, the soldiers were pushed back. Fifty-three officers and enlisted men were disabled during the first charge.

But ultimately, the Nez Perces could not withstand the superior firepower of the Army. The small remnant of cold, hungry Indians who had survived the flight surrendered to Colonel Miles.

Joseph and his followers were first sent to Fort Leavenworth, then to the Quapaw Reservation in Kansas, and finally to Indian Territory (now Oklahoma). At each place, scores of men, women, and children died. Finally, in May 1885, the Lower Nez Perce were allowed to return to the Northwest, half to the Lapwai Reservation in Idaho and half, including Joseph and his family, to the Colville Reservation in eastern Washington.

For many years, Joseph begged authorities to allow him and his band to return to the Wallowa Valley. In 1901, he exclaimed,

> My home is in the Wallowa Valley, and I want to go back there to live. My father and mother are buried there. If the government would only give me a small piece of land for my people in the Wallowa Valley, with a teacher, that is all I would ask.

Joseph waited, but federal authorities never responded. When the old chief died in 1904, he still harbored the dream that someday he might go home.

CHAPTER TWENTY-SIX

The Bloody Adventures of Harry Tracy
·1902·

June 9, 1902, started out like any other day at the Salem, Oregon, prison. Two guards, Farrell and Girard, were busy counting prisoners in the courtyard. Satisfied that they were all present and accounted for, the guards ordered the men to march to the foundry for another hard day's work.

One of the inmates, Harry Tracy, must have been a bundle of nerves. He knew that an accomplice had hidden a pair of guns in a tool box just inside the foundry door. He planned to use them to escape.

Inside the shadowy foundry, Tracy spied a tool box with chalk markings on its lid. He maintained his place in the orderly procession until he came close enough to lunge toward it. He threw open the lid and pulled out a rifle and a sawed-off shotgun.

Passing the shotgun to Dave Merrill, the prisoner in line behind him, Tracy opened fire with the rifle and shot Farrell in the head, killing him instantly. Pandemonium ensued. Before the surviving guard knew what was happening, the prisoners had flooded back into the courtyard, screaming and attacking every guard in sight.

In the confusion, Tracy and Merrill scaled the prison wall and dropped to freedom on the other side, shooting several guards along the way. According to historian James D. Horan, Tracy then vanished into the thick brush with Merrill. Behind them the sirens of the prison wailed like frenzied banshees. Telegraph and telephone wires hummed with orders. One of the greatest manhunts in American history had begun.

Just a few miles from prison, Tracy and Merrill accosted two deputy sheriffs and commandeered their horse-drawn carriage. Then they stole some more guns and headed for Portland. At Gervais, a fifty-man posse surrounded the escapees, but they managed to slip through the lawmen's fingers. By the time the pair reached Portland a few days later, the governor had called out 250 militiamen to join the search. Tracy managed to escape by forcing a local boatman to take him and Merrill across the Columbia River to Washington.

If the two believed they were safe in Washington, they had another thought coming. As they continued northward toward Tacoma, both the reward for their capture and the size of the posse grew. The governor of Washington ordered his officers to shoot to kill.

Soon after arriving at Tacoma, Merrill came to the end of his road. Tracy killed him after learning that Merrill had testified against him years earlier in exchange for a lighter prison sentence. Alone, Tracy captured a fishing craft on Puget Sound and forced its captain to carry him to Seattle. At a farmhouse there, the elusive killer once again was almost captured. He shot several more men before escaping.

Tracy now turned eastward and made his way toward Spokane. When he reached Lincoln County, he decided to hole up for a while and let the furor die down. But Tracy's luck had run out. Only a few days later the law caught up with him, this time for good.

Harry Tracy was a native of New York. In 1896, only twenty-seven years old and already wanted for murder in Utah, he joined Butch Cassidy's notorious "Wild Bunch." He felt right at home with the other gang members, among them Harry Longabaugh (the Sundance Kid), Harvey Logan, and George "Kid" Curry.

Tracy eventually was caught and imprisoned at Aspen, Colorado. Escaping soon afterward, he made his way to Oregon, where, again, he was arrested and imprisoned, this time at Salem. He had served a little over three years when he and Merrill made their daring prison break in June 1902.

During August, rumors about Tracy's whereabouts were as thick as the ripening wheat in the golden fields outside Creston, Washington. The town marshal, Charles Straub, dismissed most of the tales, but when an eyewitness claimed to have seen Tracy on a nearby farm, the lawman decided to investigate. Straub deputized four men—Oscar Lillengreen, Maurice Smith, Joe Morrison, and Dr. E.C. Lanter—and the small posse saddled up.

At the farm, the lawmen found three men working on a barn. Tracy's photograph had been all over the front pages of the local newspapers lately, and Straub noticed that one of the workers bore a striking resemblance to the fugitive. He identified himself as a law officer and ordered Tracy to surrender. Instead, the outlaw grabbed his rifle, fired a few shots, and disappeared into the billowing wheat fields that surrounded the farm.

It soon grew dark, and the five lawmen took up positions around the edges of the wheat field, where they planned to wait until morning. Sometime during the night, the posse heard a single shot. At dawn, they found Tracy dead, the victim of his own hand. They also could see that he had bled copiously from a leg wound during the night. Obviously, he had opted for a quick death rather than slowly bleed to death or be captured.

And so ended the career of the outlaw Horan once described as the "mad dog of the Wild Bunch." After a few weeks as the biggest news story in the United States, he was largely forgotten.

CHAPTER TWENTY-SEVEN

The Smashing Success of the Suffragettes

· 1912 ·

It was a proud day for Oregon women when a small group, led by seventy-eight-year-old Abigail Scott Duniway, met in the governor's office in 1912. Governor Oswald West had specifically invited Mrs. Duniway because it was due to her drive and persistence that he was about to sign a law giving Oregon women the right to vote. In fact, Duniway had contributed most of the language of the bill, and for her active part in the women's rights movement, she was invited to sign her name right next to that of the governor.

Abigail Scott had been born in Tazewell County, Illinois, in 1834. One of ten children, she was raised in a farming community. She recalled in later life how disappointed her mother had been when girls were born into the large family. "Poor baby," her mother had lamented. "She'll be a woman some day. A woman's lot is so hard!"

When Abigail was eighteen, she moved with her family to Oregon, where she got a teaching job in the small community of Lafayette. The following year, she married Benjamin Charles Duniway and began a family of her own. When he was injured in an accident and could no longer support the family, Abigail resumed teaching and then opened a prosperous millinery shop. By 1870, Abigail's experience as a small-business owner had exposed her to the obstacles women faced when trying to make a living in a man's world. She helped organize an "Equal Rights Society" in Albany, Oregon. A year later, she sold her shop and moved her family to Portland.

Duniway's next venture was a newspaper she founded, *The New Northwest*, and for the next sixteen years she devoted most of her columns to the advocacy of women's rights. Shortly after her inaugural issue hit the streets, she received a visit from the well-known suffragette, Susan B. Anthony. Duniway agreed to travel across Oregon and Washington as Anthony's business manager.

In 1883, Duniway succeeded in pursuading the Washington Territorial Legislature to give its women the right to vote. Thirteen years later, at her urging, the state of Idaho did likewise. Yet Oregon eluded her. Once, in 1884, the state had considered passing a constitutional amendment giving the vote to women. But when members of the Women's Christian Temperance Union campaigned for prohibition, liquor-loving legislators defeated the measure.

Despite Duniway's belief in equal voting rights, she still maintained that a woman's place was first and foremost in the home. In 1899, at a celebration of Oregon's fortieth anniversary of statehood, the soft-spoken suffragette told her audience:

> The interests of the sexes can never be identically the same; but they are always mutual, always interdependent, and every effort to separate them results, primarily, in discontent and ultimately in failure.... Woman is the world's homemaker, and she ought always to be its homemaker.... The woman who would neglect her family for the allurements of social frivolity, or the emoluments and honors of public life, is not the woman whose name will occupy a place among the annals of the Oregon pioneers.

However, Duniway was quick to point out the important contributions of Oregon's early homemakers. "Have they not as nobly and bravely borne their part as did the men?" she asked. "Were they not as faithful as they in building up this vigorous young commonwealth of the Pacific Northwest?"

In 1905, at the Lewis and Clark Exposition in Portland, Duniway made yet another appeal to state lawmakers. Once again, she was disappointed. Finally, in 1912, just three years before her death, the crusader saw her dream come true. With the simple stroke of a pen, Governor West bestowed upon Duniway and her spiritual sisters the right to have a say in the politics of their home state.

CHAPTER TWENTY-EIGHT

The Great Tillamook Fire
· 1933 ·

By one o'clock on August 14, 1933, most of the lumberjacks working in Gales Creek Canyon had just finished eating lunch. Because the weather was so hot and dry—there had been little rain for the past two months—the logging companies had been ordered to cease operations at noon. Although this meant the companies would get less timber out of the vast Douglas-fir forests that covered Tillamook County, all agreed it was better to conform than to risk starting a fire in the tinder-dry wilderness.

But there was one timber company that failed to be impressed by the serious danger of working in the dry forest during the hottest part of the day. So when the whistle blew at one o'clock, its crew returned to work with plans to remove a giant fir bole that had been felled before lunch.

A lumberjack known as a "chokerman," or "choker setter," attached one end of a long metal cable, the "choker," to the log. When the cable was in place, a young boy called a "punk" pulled a line connected to the nearby "donkey engine," setting off a whistle to notify the engine operator that the log was ready to move. The donkey engine was a rig that ran on gasoline and was much like a small locomotive. It generated several horsepower of pulling action, which was used to drag logs out of the forests.

The little donkey engine screamed, and the steel cable pulled taut. Slowly at first, then more rapidly as the engine revved up to full power, the giant log moved across the forest floor. With a sudden surge, the log jumped from its path and glided several yards through the air. When it landed, it collided with an old disease-ridden cedar that had blown down years earlier. The cedar was tinder-dry.

Within a minute after the log hit the ground, one of the lumberjacks standing near the dead cedar noticed smoke curling up from its trunk. One of the workers ran back to camp to warn his comrades of the potential danger, while the others began trying to put out the blaze. Only moments had passed, but it was already too late. Fire raced up and down the dead cedar and jumped to other logs lying nearby. Within minutes, the hot flames had flared out of control.

At about the same time, a forester in a lookout tower atop Saddle Mountain saw wisps of smoke. He telephoned headquarters at Forest Grove to report the fire's location. Moments later, a forester at the Hoffman lookout station called, too, and rangers were able to plot the precise location of the blaze and dispatch a crew of firefighters.

By six in the evening, the lumberjacks in Gales Creek Canyon had been joined by about one hundred firefighters. In the meantime, the blaze, driven by high, dry winds, had jumped a large portion of forest and started a new blaze along Wilson River, several miles to the south. Men from all of the commercial timber companies and nearby sawmills, as well as a crew from the Civilian Conservation Corps of Forest Grove, were loaded into trucks and rushed to the scene.

Despite efforts to contain the fire on the ground, the massive blaze crowned and sped through the treetops like the wind. More men, many from Portland, were sent to fight the blaze. For days, the battle of man against Nature continued.

By Thursday, August 24, the fire had destroyed forty thousand acres of prime Douglas-fir. Just when it looked as though the fire was under control, the humidity dropped to twenty-six percent, and a dry, hot east wind blasted across the forest. Stewart H. Holbrook, a logger at the time, was an eyewitness to the great Tillamook Burn, as the fire was called. In his book, *Burning an Empire*, he wrote

No man could tell exactly what was happening that day, but... the fire had blown up. Along a fifteen mile front a wall of flame leaped through the tops of four-hundred-year-old trees. Smoke rolled and billowed above the flames, and in Portland, that day, fifty miles away, citizens marveled and were awed at the great motionless cloud, gray-white and far bigger than any cloud they had ever seen, which seemed to hang in the sky southwest of the city.

Meanwhile, that same day, an arsonist set a fire in neighboring Clatsop County. When firefighters arrived to combat that conflagration, it, too, was out of control. By now, more than three thousand men were occupied fighting the many blazes that had spread throughout Tillamook and Clatsop counties.

Finally, Nature stepped in to offer a helping hand. A thick, wet fog rolled inland from the Pacific Ocean during the early morning of August 25, enabling firefighters to contain and eventually control the fires. Within a matter of days, more than 311,000 acres—twelve and a half billion board feet—of prime timberland had been destroyed. Put another way, enough timber was lost between August 14 and 25 to have supplied the lumber needs of every American family in the previous year!

CHAPTER TWENTY-NINE

President Roosevelt's Visit to Oregon

· 1937 ·

President Franklin D. Roosevelt beamed with pleasure as he stood before Timberline Lodge on September 28, 1937. The new building, perched on the south slope of Mount Hood, was a "monument to the skill and faithful performance of workers," he told the crowd. It was a magnificent example of government/ civilian cooperation as expressed through Roosevelt's own Works Progress Administration and Civilian Conservation Corps.

Roosevelt's visit to the lodge was part of a two-week railroad trip to the Pacific Northwest. Also on his agenda was the dedication of the almost-completed Bonneville Dam, which spanned the Columbia River between Portland and The Dalles.

It is not certain which of the early European explorers who sailed along the Oregon coastline first spied Mount Hood. The snow-clad peak was named by Captain George Vancouver in 1792, after a British naval figure. It soars 11,235 feet above the surrounding forests of Douglas-fir and pine that clothe the Cascade Mountains. The formidable peak was not scaled to its summit until 1845.

By the end of the 1800s, Mount Hood had become popular with hikers, skiers, and campers. In 1916, the U.S. Forest Service, which had jurisdiction over the peak, built "Timberline Cabin," a tiny shelter near timberline that could be used by climbers in an emergency. Eight years later, a "tent hotel" was constructed, providing such amenities as mattresses and meals for overnight guests.

In the meantime, several local outdoors groups were harboring the idea of making Mount Hood a year-round resort. When Roosevelt announced his massive public-works projects as a way to pull Americans out of the Great Depression, the time seemed right to build a permanent lodge.

In 1936, the U.S. Forest Service hired a private architect, Gilbert Stanley Underwood, to design the building. Underwood planned a massive, rustic ski lodge with three levels surrounding a huge lobby, the focal point of which would be a ninety-two-foot-high fireplace. Unemployed local people were hired to do the work. By the time the lodge was finished, more than five hundred men and women had trekked six miles up the mountain every day to get to their jobs.

A current brochure aptly describes the rustic loveliness of Timberline Lodge:

> In a state known for its rugged natural beauty, Timberline Lodge is a fitting monument to the pioneer spirit. Solidly perched at the 6,000' level of snow-capped Mt. Hood, it is the grandest example of Cascadian architecture. The Works Progress Administration (WPA) built the lodge during the Great Depression, employing hundreds of master craftsmen. Inside and out, the lodge is handmade, from its massive, hand-hewn

beams to its handwoven draperies.... Timberline Lodge is a living museum of arts and crafts inspired by pioneer, Indian, and wildlife themes.

The second chairlift in the world was installed on Mount Hood in 1939, attracting more visitors to the area. In 1972, the lodge was added to the National Register of Historic Places. Today, more than one million visitors drive up the winding road through the Mount Hood National Forest to the lodge to ski, camp, climb, or simply enjoy the impressive surroundings.

The very day of his visit to Timberline Lodge, Roosevelt took part in the dedication of the Bonneville Dam. A *Time* magazine reporter who followed the presidential party wrote in the October 11, 1937, issue that

> the President spent a week roving through the vast forests and high mountains of the most heroic terrain in the U. S. as though he had on [Paul] Bunyan's boots. Bonneville Dam, 170 ft. high, 1,250 ft. long is being built by War Department engineers complete with staircases as well as two electric elevators for traveling salmon.

At the dedication of the dam and powerhouse, Roosevelt took the opportunity to promote his public-works philosophy.

> Instead of spending, as some nations do, half their national income in piling up armaments... we in America are wiser in using our wealth on projects like this which will give us more wealth, better living and greater happiness for our children.

CHAPTER THIRTY

A Wild Night at Fort Stevens
· 1942 ·

Six months after Pearl Harbor, the soldiers at Fort Stevens, Oregon, knew exactly how vulnerable the West Coast was to a Japanese attack. Some thought it was only a matter of time before the enemy tried to invade the Pacific Northwest. So they took their job, which included guarding the strategic entrance to the Columbia River, very seriously.

The men at the fort had plenty of reasons to worry in June 1942. In February, a Japanese submarine had fired at petroleum installations near Santa Barbara, California. The Japanese had just invaded Attu and Kiska, two islands in the Aleutian chain of Alaska. And on June 20, an enemy sub had attacked a lighthouse and telegraph station on Vancouver Island.

The twenty-first of June started out like most other days at Fort Stevens. The men went about their daily chores, patroling the beach, swabbing out latrines, and tinkering with the big cannons and mortars that made up the armament of most of the batteries at the fort. But shortly before midnight, the routine was shattered. The soldiers were awakened by the unmistakable sound of an artillery round screaming overhead. Then they heard the loud boom as the shell exploded on the beach.

In the next fifteen minutes, another sixteen rounds of artillery exploded nearby. The soldiers were frantic. Leaping from their bunks, many of them manned their battle stations in nothing but their helmets and underwear. They prepared the big guns for action and waited for the order to fire.

To their dismay, the order never came. The head of the

Harbor Defense Command had decided that, since the enemy had not hit anything important with its first barrage, it would be foolish to fire back and betray the location of the U.S. guns.

The Japanese were jubilant about their offensive. Years after the incident, Meiji Tagami, the submarine commander who ordered the shelling, recalled that

> the first shot was like an electric shock to the crew.... They shouted and danced about on the deck hugging one another; one crew member hugged me and my face was sore from the scratching of his unshaven face.

There was no joy at Fort Stevens, however. The men, eager to fight, could only watch and wait. Fortunately, as night turned into day, no further incidents occurred. In the light of dawn, the solders could see that the fort had sustained no damage. The shells had fallen harmlessly on the beach or in the swamp behind the fort.

The attack on Fort Stevens had happened too late to make the local newspapers the following day. But on Tuesday, June 23, *The Oregonian* gave its readers full coverage of what had been the first attack on a mainland U.S. military installation since the War of 1812. "Fort Stevens Target of Jap Submarine's Guns," the headlines proclaimed. "9 Shells Scream Ashore On Oregon Coast; Army Announces Damage Nil." Original stories of the attack mistakenly reported that only nine rounds had been fired. But later investigation showed that seventeen shells had hit the coast.

The submarine responsible for the assault escaped and so was able to take part in yet another attack on Oregon. On two occasions in September, a plane launched from its deck dropped incendiary bombs over the forests east of Cape Blanco, near the California border. But in late August 1943, fate caught up with the submarine. It was destroyed in the South Pacific by the U.S. Navy.

Japan's plan to invade and occupy the Aleutian Islands—and perhaps the Pacific Northwest as well—was short-lived. The defeat suffered by the Imperial Navy at the Battle of Midway in

June 1942 crippled Japanese seapower. The loss of 3,500 men, four aircraft carriers, and three hundred aircraft spelled the beginning of the end for Emperor Hirohito's Japanese empire.

A few days after the attack on Fort Stevens, one of the soldiers succinctly expressed his buddies' feelings when he hung a sign on one of the fences surrounding the post. It read, "9 Shots Fired, 9 Shots Missed, To Hell With Hirohito."

CHAPTER THIRTY-ONE

The Legacy of Hells Canyon
·1976·

On July 31, 1976—four weeks after millions of proud Americans celebrated the U.S. Bicentennial—about three hundred people assembled for another special occasion at Hat Point on the Oregon rim of Hells Canyon. On this sunny, hot day, the group would dedicate Hells Canyon National Recreation Area, bringing into reality what had long been the dream of many.

Speakers for the occasion relied heavily on superlatives in describing the yawning chasm carved by the Snake River. U.S. Senator Robert Packwood of Oregon referred to it as "the jewel that is Hells Canyon." Congressman Al Ullman, also of Oregon, called it "the most beautiful area in the world." And Governor Bob Straub termed it "magnificent" and "incomparable."

Though the canyon was the focus of admiration that summer day, it had for decades been a battleground where various factions had wrestled for the right to control its future. One private group, the Pacific Northwest Power Company, had wanted to build a dam across the Snake at Pittsburg Landing. When the Federal Power Commission rejected that site, Pacific Northwest proposed another just above the confluence of the Snake and the Salmon rivers. Another faction favored building a dam at Nez Perce.

Meanwhile, someone discovered that the annual salmon runs had been adversely affected by the fish-passage equipment at the Oxbow Dam, farther upstream. When the salmon lobby entered the fray with a demand that *no* dam be built across the Snake, the situation got even more complicated. And when the

Federal Power Commission approved Pacific Northwest's second request, the Washington Public Power Supply System, a consortium of several regional utility companies, filed suit and successfully blocked the construction.

The case reached the U.S. Supreme Court, and on June 5, 1967, Justice William O. Douglas, who hailed from neighboring Washington, issued his opinion. He stressed that the issue was not

> solely whether the region will be able to use the electric power. The test is whether the project will be in the public interest. And that determination can be made only after an exploration of all issues relevant to the "public interest," including future power demand and supply, alternate sources of power, the public interest in preserving reaches of rivers and wilderness areas, the preservation of anadromous fish for commercial and recreational purposes, and the protection of wildlife.

When Packwood was elected to the U.S. Senate, he advocated the preservation of pristine Hells Canyon. Through the combined efforts of the Sierra Club and members of the Oregon and Idaho congressional delegations, legislation was passed that prevented damming of the stretch of the Snake that ran through Hells Canyon. President Gerald Ford signed the act creating the Hells Canyon National Recreational Area on December 31, 1975.

Today, Hells Canyon National Recreational Area is a 215,000-acre wilderness that preserves a sixty-seven-mile stretch of the Snake River. Adorned with ancient Indian petroglyphs, the canyon walls stretch upward almost eight thousand feet in some places, making Hells Canyon the deepest gorge on the face of the earth.

CHAPTER THIRTY-TWO

A Potpourri of Oregon Facts

• Oregon is the tenth largest state in the nation. It encompasses 97,073 square miles, or more than 62 million acres. It averages 345 miles from east to west, and 278 miles from north to south.

• The mean elevation of Oregon is 3,300 feet. The highest point in the state is Mount Hood, in the Cascade Mountains, with an altitude of 11,237 feet. The lowest point in the state is sea level on the Pacific Coast.

• The geographical center of Oregon is a point twenty-five miles southeast of Prineville in Crook County.

• The latest agricultural statistics (1991) show that Oregon contains about 37,000 farms totaling about 18 million acres, an average of 486 acres per farm.

• The 1990 census showed that Oregon's population was 2,842,000. The estimated 1991 population was 2,922,000, or thirty people per square mile.

• The state ranks 29th in the nation for population.

• The coldest temperature ever recorded in Oregon was minus 54 degrees Fahrenheit on February 10, 1933, at Seneca.

• The hottest temperature was 119 degrees on August 10, 1898, at Pendleton.

• Oregon became a U.S. Territory in 1848. It became the thirty-third state on February 14, 1859.

• Salem, with a population in 1990 of 108,000, is the capital of Oregon.

• Portland, with a population in 1990 of 437,319, is the state's largest city.

• Oregon contains thirty-six counties.

• The name Oregon may be derived from *ouragan*, a French-Canadian word for "storm" or "hurricane." The Columbia was originally called the Oregon River, perhaps because of its turbulence.

• The state motto is "The Union."

• Oregon's official state nickname is the "Beaver State."

• The state bird is the western meadowlark (*Sturnella neglecta*).

- The state flower is the Oregon grape (*Berberis aquifolium*), and the state tree is the Douglas-fir (*Pseudotsuga menziesii*).

- The state mammal is the beaver (*Castor canadensis*).

- The state insect is the Oregon swallowtail (*Papilio oregonius*).

- The state rock is the thunderegg or geode.

- The state gemstone is sunstone.

- The state fish is the chinook salmon (*Oncorhynchus tschawytscha*).

- The state song is "Oregon, My Oregon," lyrics by J.A. Buchanan and music by Henry B. Murtagh.

- The state flag consists of the state seal in gold on a navy blue field, with the words "State of Oregon" in gold above the seal and "1859" below the seal. A gold beaver adorns the reverse side.

Bibliography

Antich, Felix E. "The Night They Fired on Oregon," in *Oregon Coast Magazine*. June-July, 1984.

Ashworth, William. "Hells Canyon: Man, Land, and History in the Deepest Gorge on Earth," in *American Heritage Magazine*, Volume XXVIII, Number 3. New York: American Heritage Publishing Company, Inc., 1977.

Biddle, Nicholas, ed. *The Journals of the Expedition Under the Command of Capts. Lewis and Clark*. New York: The Heritage Press, 1962. A reprint of the history of the expedition as published in 1814 in Philadelphia.

Bowles, Samuel. *Across the Continent: A Summer's Journey to the Rocky Mountains, the Mormons, and the Pacific States, with Speaker Colfax*. Springfield, Massachusetts: Samuel Bowles & Company, 1865.

Brandon, William. "Wilson Price Hunt," in *The Mountain Men and the Fur Trade of the Far West*, Volume 6. Glendale, California: The Arthur H. Clark Company, 1968.

Burnett, Peter, H. *Recollections and Opinions of an Old Pioneer*. New York: 1880.

Dillon, Richard H. *North American Indian Wars*. New York: Facts on File, Inc., 1983.

Dryden, Cecil. *Up the Columbia for Furs*. Caldwell, Idaho: The Caxton Printers, Ltd., 1949.

Duniway, Abigail Scott. "Woman in Oregon History," in *Fortieth Anniversary of the Statehood of Oregon.* Salem, Oregon: W.H. Leeds, State Printer, 1899.

Edwards, P.L. *Sketch of the Oregon Territory or, Emigrants' Guide.* Liberty, Missouri: Printed at the "Herald" Office, 1842.

Gillette, P.W. "A Brief History of the Oregon Steam Navigation Company," in *Oregon Historical Quarterly,* Volume V, Number 2. Salem: Oregon Historical Society, 1904.

Holbrook, Stewart H. *Burning an Empire.* New York: The Macmillan Company, 1944.

The Columbia River. New York: Holt, Rinehart and Winston, 1965.

Holden, Jan. "The Varied Life of Joaquin Miller," in *The National Tombstone Epitaph,* Volume XVIII, No. 6, June 1991.

Holmes, Kenneth L. *Ewing Young; Master Trapper.* Portland: Binfords & Mort, Publishers, 1967.

Horan, James D., and Paul Sann. *Pictorial History of the Wild West.* New York: Crown Publishers, Inc., 1954.

Irving, Washington. *Astoria, or Anecdotes of an Enterprise Beyond the Rocky Mountains.* Philadelphia: Carey, Lea, & Blanchard, 1836.

Jackson, Donald, and Mary Lee Spence, eds. *The Explorations of John Charles Fremont.* Volume 1. Urbana: University of Illinois Press, 1970.

Karolevitz, Robert F. *Newspapering in the Old West.* Seattle: Superior Publishing Company, 1965. Reprinted by Bonanza

Books, New York, nd.

Kastner, Joseph. *A Species of Eternity.* New York: E.P. Dutton, 1977.

Lavender, David. *Let Me Be Free.* New York: HarperCollins Publishers, 1992.

The Way to the Western Sea. New York: Harper & Row, Publishers, 1988.

Lindstrom, David. *The Japanese Submarine, I-25, and the Oregon Coast.* Hammond, Oregon: Fort Stevens State Park, 1992.

Lomax, Alfred L. *Pioneer Woolen Mills in Oregon.* Portland: Binfords & Mort, Publishers, 1941.

Lovejoy, A.L. "Lovejoy's Pioneer Narrative," in *Oregon Historical Quarterly*, Volume XXXI, Number 3. Salem: Oregon Historical Society, 1930.

Mark, Frederick A. "The Bannack Indian War of 1878," in *Great Western Indian Fights.* Lincoln: University of Nebraska Press, 1960.

Morgan, Dale. *Jedediah Smith and the Opening of the West.* Indianapolis: The Bobbs-Merrill Company, Inc., 1953.

Moulton, Gary E., ed. *The Journals of the Lewis & Clark Expedition*, Volume 6. Lincoln: University of Nebraska Press, 1990.

Our National Parks. Pleasantville, N.Y.: The Reader's Digest Association, Inc., 1985.

Peterson, Roger Tory, and James Fisher. *Wild America*. Boston: Houghton Mifflin Company, 1955.

Porter, Kenneth W. "Jane Barnes, First White Woman in Oregon," in *Oregon Historical Quarterly*, Volume XXXI, No. 2. Salem, Oregon: Oregon Historical Society, 1930.

Reiter, Joan Swallow. *The Women*. Alexandria, Virginia: Time-Life Books, 1978.

"Remme's Great Ride," in *American Heritage Magazine*, Volume XXIV, Number 1. New York: American Heritage Publishing Company, Inc., 1972.

Scott, Leslie M. "Beginnings of East Portland," in *Oregon Historical Quarterly*, Volume XXXI, Number 4. Salem: Oregon Historical Society, 1930.

"Pioneer Gold Money, 1849," in *Oregon Historical Quarterly*, Volume XXXIII, Number 1. Salem: Oregon Historical Society, 1932.

Timberland Lodge: An Expression of Hope and Purpose. Washington, D.C.: U.S. Forest Service, 1992.

Time magazine. October 11, 1937.

Townsend, John K. *Narrative of a Journey across the Rocky Mountains to the Columbia River*. Philadelphia: Henry Perkins, 1839. Partially reprinted in Anderson, Sylvia F., and Jacob Korg, eds. *Westward to Oregon*. Boston: D.C. Heath and Company, 1958.

Utley, Robert M., and Wilcomb E. Washburn. *The American Heritage History of the Indian Wars*. New York: American Heritage Publishing Company, 1977.

Vestal, Stanley. *Joe Meek: The Merry Mountain Man.* Lincoln: University of Nebraska Press, 1963.

Viola, Herman J., and Carolyn Margolis, eds. *Magnificent Voyagers: The U.S. Exploring Expedition, 1838-1842.* Washington, D.C.: Smithsonian Institution Press, 1985.

Williams, Richard L. *The Loggers.* Alexandria, Virginia: Time-Life Books, 1976.

The Wool Story... From Fleece to Fashion. Portland: Pendleton Woolen Mills, 1991.

Index

ENED IN

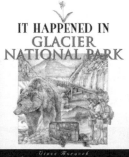

IT HAPPENED IN
GLACIER
NATIONAL PARK

IT HAPPENED IN
MAINE

IT HAPPENED ON THE
OREGON TRAIL

Written in a lively, easy-to-read style that is entertaining as well as informative, the **IT HAPPENED IN** series presents the most captivating moments in the nation's history. These books appeal to history buffs of all ages.

Books in the IT HAPPENED IN series include:

Arizona	Montana	Revolutionary War
Cape Cod	Nevada	San Francisco
Civil War	New Hampshire	South Carolina
Colorado	New Jersey	Southern California
Florida	New Mexico	Tennessee
Georgia	New York	Texas
Glacier National Park	North Carolina	Utah
Great Smokies	Northern California	Virginia
Idaho	Oregon	Washington
Lewis and Clark Expedition	Oregon Trail	Washington, D.C.
Maine	Outer Banks	Yellowstone
Massachusetts	Pennsylvania	

TWODOT®

TwoDot® is an imprint of
The Globe Pequot Press

For a complete listing of all our titles, please visit our Web site at www.GlobePequot.com.

Available wherever books are sold.

Orders can also be placed on the Web at www.GlobePequot.com, by phone from 8:00 A.M. to 5:00 P.M. at 1-800-243-0495, or by fax at 1-800-820-2329.